THE WAY BACK HOME

essays on life and family

Peggy O'Mara

MOTHERING
PUBLICATIONS
Santa Fe, New Mexico

This book is dedicated to Ruth and Oliver, my first loves.

Many of the essays in this book originally appeared in
Mothering magazine between 1983 and 1991. All previously
published material has been reedited for this edition by Peggy
O'Mara, Ellen Kleiner, and Richard Harris.

© 1991 by Peggy O'Mara
First edition. First printing

Published by Mothering, PO Box 1690, Santa Fe, NM 87504
Printed in the United States of America

Cover design by Mary Shapiro
Front cover photograph by Ron Meyer
Back cover photograph by Eric Swanson

ISBN 0-914257-09-9

Contents

Introduction

A s I was writing these essays over the last nine years, I did not see them as the whole that they form here. They were bits and pieces of life, some written for deadlines, some exploding out of me. Originally I gave them very little space, cramming the words into two columns on a magazine page. It was Gail Grenier Sweet, one of *Mothering*'s first Contributing Editors, who suggested that I give them more room, and so they grew to two pages. My friend Ashisha began to illustrate them, and eventually I was brave enough to use my photograph with them.

I learned to write in the fire. Some of the essays—most of the early ones—were written with children underfoot and with countless interruptions. I didn't know there was another way, so I learned to write amid the fracas. Later, as my children grew up and my opinion of myself improved, I gave myself quiet time, and my writing took on new polish. At that point, my essays were given the title "A Quiet Place," after the quotation "I am myself a quiet place."

The inspirations and philosophies that now seem to flow so coherently through these essays were pieced together from the grit of daily life. They were my practical solutions for living a family life that I had no model for. They are about me, not about what I think you "should" do. Writing, for me, is a synthesis of a burning inner dilemma. When I write, I bring together numerous disparate thoughts into something that makes sense to me and that I can live with. While I have always been pleased when others enjoy my essays, it has never been my intent to proselytize.

I like my children, and I have wanted to be with them. I immersed myself in family because I needed to do so for my own healing and because the role of mother was the only female role with which I felt unconflicted. I lost myself as a person through this immersion in mothering and in becoming a spokesperson for mothers. And I found my way back. That's what these essays are about.

They are about finding our way back to valuing the family, to valuing relationship, and finding our way back to ourselves from which all our relationships stem. I believe that never before in history have men and women experienced genuine friendship with one another, told each other what each wants in relationship, and tried so hard to keep the balance between self and other. I also believe that never before in history have children been seen as real people with independent needs of their own—needs that parents and society have a responsibility to address.

My personal ideals and the task of translating my experience to others have been great motivators for me. As Nancy Griffith sings, "There are some who can't love right; I just can't love wrong." I've had to make it work.

The reason I am so idealistic is not because I am naïve about the economic and personal challenges of society of today, but because I am so stubborn. I have refused to be dictated to by others' ideas of who I "should" be or what my life "should" look like. As Joseph Campbell encouraged, "Follow your bliss." Do that which helps you feel happy inside. And do it not because it is the new way or because it gives meaning to life, but because it is life. By really *experiencing* life, you are truly alive.

I am not interested in transcending life or in rising above it. I like my body, and I want to jump with it off the bridge of life, blindfolded with both eyes open. I want to get a running start, and I want my children to get a running start. Life has buffeted me around quite a bit. I've had my share of suffering. Death has been in my neighborhood from time to time, and I have known hopelessness. And I have managed to get up again and stand on my own two feet. Not because I am more virtuous or exceptional than the next person, but because it is the only way to survive.

I am a pragmatist. Most of my ideals and my philosophy about being a parent are simply practical solutions. When I homeschooled, I didn't have to get up in the morning. When I breastfed, I didn't have to go to the kitchen to make bottles in the middle of the night. When I took my babes to bed with me, I could get back to sleep sooner. When I started getting funny with my teenagers, I could talk to them. When I left my marriage, I stayed alive.

By surrendering into what I really am rather than trying to be more than what I am, I found myself. When you read my words, please remember that I am not perfect either. I am in the middle of the fray, and I know how to make pretty words. These essays are about the ideas that have kept my spirits high and my resolve up when those around me were telling me that everything I believed in was impossible. I hope you will find your own practical solutions, whatever they may be. I know that if they are your own solutions, you will never regret them, even if things don't work out the way you hope they will. Value yourself and the ones you love. Love your neighbor. And leave the rest to God.

Growing Healthy Families

I t can seem as though we are without rules and guideposts to point the way in parenting. We read about the demise of the family, the deterioration of family life and of society. We hear about high crime rates, increased violence, and the new age of impersonal technology. Amid this bombardment of bad news about interpersonal relationships, we wonder if there is any way to raise the kind of emotionally and physically healthy children we want to raise. We love our children, but society gives little importance to the role of parent. If our children end up in jail, it will certainly be considered our fault. If, on the other hand, they grow up to be successful and productive human beings, few will give us credit. And yet, we know that our parenting will make a difference.

We know that there must be traits of healthy families we can examine and learn from, but is it possible to put this healthiness into words? How can we gain the confidence needed to consider ourselves the professionals that we are? How can we become the experts concerning our own families, their needs and their priorities?

Parenthood is *not* a hit-and-miss operation. Certainly, much about human nature is still a mystery to us. Why do some people survive childhood traumas while others do not? Individual differences and sensitivities come into play; luck and grace must be considered. But there is, nonetheless, a body of psychological, anthropological, and sociological literature concerning emotionally stable human beings that is not mysterious. A major factor raised in this body of literature is the importance of love. We know that love is important. We all love our children. But what is love? Love is more than a feeling. Love is an action, a commitment, a conscious decision. It is this successful translation of love from feeling into action that defines why some families work and others do not.

One of the prerequisites for loving others is that we love ourselves. If we have not been well loved as children, we must work on our concepts of self-worth and self-love in adulthood and take every opportunity to grow in appreciation of ourselves. We must reach out to others who can help us expand our ability to love. We must reprogram ourselves to love ourselves better. Every time we have a demeaning thought about ourselves, we must remember something good about ourselves. We must learn not to define ourselves by our accomplishments, but to love ourselves simply for being the unique individuals that we are. From this conscious attempt to appreciate ourselves and to grow as spiritual beings will come the self-love needed to love our children.

Our journey with our children is a unique opportunity to relive our own childhoods, for at each stage of our child's life, we reexperience that same stage of our own lives. That, too, is why some stages of a child's life are more difficult than others, and why we seem to overreact to certain types of behaviors. To grow healthy families, we must begin with ourselves. We must welcome every parenting opportunity as a chance to reflect on the values and beliefs that we may have inherited from our families of birth but that may no longer fit our current personalities. We must remember that as human beings, it is our nature and our purpose to be dynamically growing and changing. Even though natural inertia and laziness may tell us that we cannot improve or that progress will be too difficult, it is always worth our best efforts to grow with our children.

How do we translate the love we have for our children into action? One way is through loving messages. Pam Levin, in her book *Becoming the Way We Are: A Transactional Guide to Personal*

Development (Berkeley, CA: Transactional Publications, 1974), gives some suggestions on this approach. She suggests that from birth on, we all need to hear five loving messages: You have every right to be here, Your needs are OK with me, I'm glad you're a boy or I'm glad you're a girl, You don't have to hurry, and I like to hold you.

We can convey these messages to our children in the ways we talk to them, touch them, and play with them. "I'm glad you're a boy or a girl" has nothing to do with sexism, and everything to do with affirming that your child's gender is a precious component of who she or he is. "You don't have to hurry" affirms that each particular stage of growth is a good one and need not be hurried through to please others. "It is good that you are crawling." "It is good that you are walking." "It is good that you are a teenager." None of these states is better than any other, nor is it important to do one sooner or better than other children in order to be a good person. Each particular person's pace is to be respected, and we can give our children this important message early on in life.

We can also help ourselves believe these important messages by visualizing our children as the emotionally healthy beings we know they are but sometimes lose sight of. When my daughter was seriously ill, for example, I would look at her and say to myself, "I see you as God sees you—strong, healthy, and wise, with plenty to meet your every need."

Ross Campbell, in his book *How to Really Love Your Child* (Wheaton, Illinois: Victor Books, 1980), reminds us that parents must have a basic love bond with their child. The only kind of love that is truly affirming and self-esteem-producing is unconditional love. Our love for our children cannot be dependent upon what they do. If we express love to our children only when they please us, we are really only loving ourselves by reassuring ourselves of our own values and beliefs. As the adult in the parent-child relationship, we must risk self-doubt and insecurity by loving our children even when their behavior is emotionally threatening to us. After all, the biting child or the hitting child is more in need of love than the child who does not misbehave; and to withhold that love, either overtly or covertly, can damage the child's self-esteem. A child's work is to experiment, to learn to resolve conflict by having conflict with others. The parent's unconditional love during these difficult periods enables the child to reflect back the unconditional love he or she has known and to maintain high self-esteem.

Loving our children no matter what they do is not the same as forsaking discipline or accepting any behavior. We can dislike the deed without disliking the doer, and we can make this distinction when responding to unacceptable behaviors. Discipline follows naturally from a solid parent-child love bond if the parents are good listeners, focus their attention on their children, learn different ways of expressing anger, and realize that the child who misbehaves is a red beacon pointing to unfulfilled emotional needs.

How often we use eye contact and focused attention while reprimanding our children. How often we withdraw eye contact when we are mad at them. Withdrawing eye contact is a very real way of withdrawing love. Instead, we should use eye contact while actively listening to our children; we should get down to their level, look them right in the eyes, and give them our full physical attention and mental focus. This one habit can do more to improve your relationship with your children (and your partner) and heighten their self-esteem than you can imagine.

Focusing attention on your child is a way of telling her that she is valued, important, and worthy of attention. Toys, gum, and even healthy food can't substitute for focused attention. There is no substitute. And focused attention takes time—one of the most precious gifts we can give our children.

We need to find time to spend alone with our children. This means establishing personal priorities and not being consumed by obligations outside the home, being willing to let the phone ring sometimes (taking it off the hook during dinnertime and storytime), being willing to say no to obligations that interfere with family togetherness, and making and keeping "appointments" with family members—by making daily conscious choices to put family first.

We all know how easy it is to give physical contact to a nursing baby. One of the lovely things about breastfeeding, and what makes it such a wonderful mothering tool, is that it ensures focused attention, eye contact, and physical touching. As our children get older, we experience physical affection in other ways: through hugging, kissing, touching a shoulder, tousling hair, gentle poking, stroking, wrestling, holding hands, putting an arm around a shoulder, back-rubbing, foot-rubbing, massage. Maintaining physical contact may be difficult because of our cultural distrust of touching and the lack of modeling in our own upbringing. If we didn't come from a touching family, we may have to learn new ways to touch our older children and consciously remember to convey our love to them physically.

While facing the difficulties of maintaining a healthy family life, we may romanticize the past, and imagine that family life was better in "the good old days." What *was* easier was that family members had to band together to ensure their physical and economic survival. While this shared purpose did much to cement familial dependency, even the Ingalls and the Waltons had their problems. Difficulties are a reality of life, not a reflection of a family's shortcomings; in fact, the ability to admit to difficulties and deal with them is a major sign of family health. For some reason, we want to believe that a good family has no problems, that bad things don't happen to good people; but this is not so. A healthy family may have great problems, and the way they band together to face them is a measure of their emotional health as a family.

Concern for the future of the family is not new. In 1934, a government study predicted the death of the family. Children of 200 years ago were routinely wet-nursed and were little more than servants in the eyes of their families. For centuries before that, they were sent to be fostered in other families, or they were sold and traded. Even in our own century, child labor laws had to be enacted to protect youngsters from unscrupulous people. We have come a long way in upgrading the status of children. Although we have far to go in our society to fully respect the uniqueness of childhood, things do get better with each generation. Psychotherapist M. Scott Peck says in his book, *The Road Less Traveled* (New York: Simon and Schuster, 1978), that he has never known a child who was not more mentally healthy than his parents.

In a wonderful book entitled *Traits of a Healthy Family* (Minneapolis, MN: Winston Press, 1983), Dolores Curran reveals the results of a comprehensive study on the traits of healthy families. Based on the observations of 551 educators, religious workers, health workers, family counselors, and others who work regularly with families, she has established 15 traits shared by healthy families.

The number one trait is the ability to communicate and listen. Interestingly enough, literature on marriage reveals that this quality has only been considered important during the past 40 years. Healthy families communicate by listening well and responding, recognizing nonverbal messages, encouraging individual feelings and independent thinking, recognizing turn-off and put-down phrases, and developing a pattern of reconciliation. Healthy families value communication between the parents, as well as table time and conversation, which they use for positive sharing rather than for unburdening anger. These families limit or eliminate the time spent around television while eating.

Healthy families teach respect for others through example. The parents model respect by showing consideration for each other and insisting on consideration toward all family members. Individual differences within the family are honored, self-

respect is encouraged, and respect for those outside of the family is fostered. All groups of people are respected.

Healthy families share decision making with children in
accordance with their capabilities. Parents do not abdicate decision-making responsibility in the name of democracy; nor do
they make final decisions that impact on the entire family.
*Troubled families either don't allow any decision making by the chil-
dren, allow too much, or <u>cause</u> individuals to feel guilty for making
decisions.*

The healthy family develops a sense of trust. Members know
they are loved. This trust begins in the early hours of life. As
psychologist Erik Erikson says, "The infant's first social
achievement is his willingness to let the mother out of his sight
without undue anxiety or rage because she has become an inner
as well as an outer predictability." This sense of trust and
expectation of intimacy comes from the predictability and
assurance of the mother's presence during the early months
and years.

Dolores Curran notes that the professionals she surveyed
found that the healthier the family was, the more likely one
parent had remained home full-time during the early infancy of
the children. As Ashley Montagu writes, "The ability to love,
and also to respond to love, has its origin in the experience of
maternal love during infancy and early childhood—and the
inability to love, except as an act of aggression, results from the
absence of the primal bond and the frustration of that human
need. In matters of the heart, not only is it better to give than to
receive; it is essential to give *in order* to receive—for it is only
the lovable, or the caring, who will be cared about."

One of the greatest gifts we can give our children is to spend
time with them. In spending time with them, we develop trust;
provide plenty of focused attention, eye contact, and touching;
and learn to know our children well enough to understand
what type of discipline and guidance they need.

Lack of time and feeling pressured for time are great enemies

of the healthy family. Today, we tend to value ourselves by
what we *do*. Washing the dishes, making the beds, decorating
the house, and shopping for food somehow don't count. We
feel a compulsion to work, engage in cultural activities, see the
latest movies and television shows, keep up with current
events, attend service activities and religious functions, educate
ourselves, take classes, keep in shape physically by jogging or
going to the spa, be involved in soccer or scouts or 4-H, and
demonstrate against nuclear weapons and world hunger.
Perhaps we are trying too hard to fulfill cultural dictates about
what we should be doing. Or perhaps we are applying outmoded models of what we could do before children to what we can
do as a parent. Isn't it enough to have intense human relationships with family members day in and day out, to be consciously honest and loving in all our relations with them? Must this
striving be squeezed in between the carpools and other commitments that run our lives?

To have healthy families, we must learn to be in charge of our
lives. This means learning not to blame every moment of
unproductivity on family demands. It means setting priorities
and being selective in what we do outside the home. In short, it
means protecting family life. In response to every new activity,
ask yourself the following questions: "Why do I want this activity?" "How will it affect family life?" "Is it worth it?" One of the
hardest tasks of healthy family members is learning how to say
"No."

Healthy families recognize the need for play and humor.
They are aware of stress levels, and perceive illness, insomnia,
or misbehavior as an indication that the family has reached its
stress level and needs to slow down.

The healthy family likes to laugh. Norman Cousins, in his
book *Anatomy of an Illness,* describes how he cured himself of a
terminal illness through the use of humor. He brought old Marx
Brothers' movies into his hospital room and watched them
every day. I like to read James Thurber stories when I am anx-

ious or worried. Research shows that people who laugh experience less stress. Humor is a tremendous boon to physical health. Laughter steps up the pulse rate, activates muscles, enervates the circulation of blood, and increases oxygen intake—all of which promote remarkable relaxation.

The healthy family fosters responsibility and exhibits a sense of shared responsibility. As Eda LeShan says, "Becoming responsible adults is no longer a matter of whether children hang up their pajamas or put dirty towels in the hamper, but whether they care about themselves and others—and whether they see everyday chores as related to how we treat this planet."

How difficult it can be to make the transition from parenting a baby, whose wants and needs are the same, to fostering the personal responsibility of a toddler. While it is easier to pick up the toys because you want to leave, to clean up the cupboard because it is time to prepare a meal and you want your child out of the kitchen, to make the beds "the right way" because the mess is unbearable, it is definitely not better for the child. We may have to release our standards of perfect cleanliness to give our children the freedom to grow into responsible adults. Many of our mothers believed that to love is to do for; but in reality, to love *is* to let our children do *for themselves*, for only in this way can they become independent. Teaching our children that they need other people to wash their hair, dress them properly and tastefully, or feed them imposes needless handicaps. Surely our children will need extra help at times, as we all do, but our responsibility as parents is to allow our children to grow toward independence.

The healthy family realizes that fostering responsibility raises self-esteem, and that responsibility extends beyond doing daily chores to safeguarding the feelings that arise in family life. When responsibility is geared to age and ability, children live the consequences of irresponsibility. As tempting as it is to bail our children out, to remove the unpleasantness that may accompany their first attempts at being responsible, we must resist. If we hover over our children and do not allow them to learn from their misjudgments, they will miss out on valuable lessons—lessons that are better learned in the safety of family life than on their own as adults.

The healthy family teaches a sense of right and wrong. For some families, these morals have a traditional religious base; for others, they do not. Regardless of spiritual inclinations, healthy families provide clear and specific guidelines about right and wrong living. Adults in the family agree on important values, and the children are held responsible for their own behavior. Parents help their children live morally. Sometimes, in an attempt to be democratic, nondirective, and nonauthoritarian, we do not share our beliefs with our children; as parents and adults, however, it is our obligation to share our values and teach our morals so that our children have a basis on which to operate in the world. We can give them the freedom to question these values and morals later in life, but in the early years we cast them adrift in a valueless world without the foundation of our experience and personal philosophies.

There is great hope for families today. We can identify and model many attributes and ideas in our search to grow as a family. Rather than seeing this time as the demise of the family, we must realize that *this is perhaps the best time to be a family.* Increasingly, society is appreciating the value of the family, and more support and information is available to families than ever before. If we learn to trust our children, and through them to trust our own instincts as professional parents, and if we learn our limitations and when to ask for help, we are well on the way to growing truly healthy families.

4 AM God Feeding

It's interesting and sometimes frustrating to look around at women with their first babies and to see them having the classic difficulties that I have had, that other mothers I know have had, and that all contemporary mothers have had. Mothers unfortunately don't always confide in one another and hence don't realize that *all* mothers have similar problems. As a result, women often feel alone in their problems, believe there is no solution because they themselves can't think of one, and decide they must thus take drastic measures to alleviate their mothering dilemma. In failing to reach out to other mothers, they can fall short of their own high expectations for themselves.

With only one child, it is impossible to get a true perspective on the mothering experience. And so it becomes imperative to reach out to other, more experienced mothers, not because they have it "all together"—although they may appear to from a first-time mother's perspective—but simply because they have *been there*. Their ideas and suggestions, sometimes simply their conversation, will relieve the worries that often build in the middle of the night, or from lack of sleep, or lack of community support for childraising practices that are different from the norm.

Many conflicts arise in the first year of a first baby's life. Although these conflicts continue to arise in later years and with other children, they are much more dramatic in the beginning. Finding support is a big issue. Learning to turn a deaf ear to friends and relatives who don't approve, and finding new

friends who do can be challenging. And the long internal dia-
logue on one's relationship with one's own family can be difficult at a stage when life is already emotionally draining.

Time becomes an issue. One doesn't have any! Intervals that
do appear get piddled away out of fear of interruption and
because there is so much to do that one doesn't know where to
begin. Bombarded by media images of the total woman as one
who "brings home the bacon, cooks it up in a pan, and never,
ever lets her husband forget he's a man," women have to look
hard to find new images of women as mothers and of mothering as a worthwhile way of life.

This lack of self-esteem often leads to a separation of the
mother-child bond. Do I need to be alone? Does my child need
to be with other children? Again, images abound to support
these views, although in the heart of every mother who allows
herself to experience mothering fully, these assumptions are
questioned. Why are our most needy and precious ones, our
children, expected to fend for themselves before they have had
a chance to experience and outgrow dependency? Why don't
we continue to see our children's wants and needs for intimacy
as one and the same?

I find it particularly interesting and ironic that spiritual quest
has become so popular in the last several years. People pay
hundreds of dollars to attend Insight, est, Mind Control, ad
infinitum. They learn meditation and sit for hours to still their
minds. Why is it that to rise gladly at 4:00 am to meditate and
meet one's God is considered a religious experience, and yet to
rise at 4:00 am to serve the needs of one's helpless child is considered the ultimate in deprivation?

Mothering a child is the greatest act of service one can do. It
is an act of surrender, an act of love, and thus an act of God.
One can learn sitting meditation by rocking and nursing a little
one to sleep; one can learn reclining meditation by staying still
to avoid disturbing a little one who has been awake for hours;
and one can learn walking meditation by walking and swaying

with a little one who would like to be asleep for hours. One *must* learn to breathe deeply in a relaxed and meditative manner in order to still the mind that doubts one's strength to go on, that sees every speck of dust on the floor and wants to clean it, and that tempts one to be up and about the busyness of accomplishments.

Mothering a child is a tremendous opportunity for the true spiritual growth that comes from sacrifice, discipline, contemplation, and love. Nothing is more real or more relentless or more challenging than the personal growth and suffering experienced in becoming a parent. We can turn our backs on the intensity of the experience and seek spiritual growth through more popular and expensive means; but for those who care to plunge into the experience and meet it head on, to accept everything, no matter how difficult, and to trust that the love of the child will show us how to survive the ordeal and come out a better person—for those people, motherhood and fatherhood can be a most rewarding and authentic spiritual quest.

Protecting Family Life

As parents, it is important to recognize the ways in which we replenish ourselves and the conditions under which we fall apart. Being conscious of both extremes, and encouraging the first while avoiding the second, helps us handle the sometimes overwhelming need our children have for us. In the beginning, that need is for pure energy—holding, touching, nursing, kissing, carrying. The need arises every time a baby and parent are together. As our children get older, however, their needs become more mental and emotional. Focused attention, eye contact, and concentrated times of togetherness for talking and exchanging questions become especially important as children outgrow the period of intense physical contact. In many ways, caring gets more challenging as our children grow up.

Emotional connection and relationship in the home lay the foundation for future relationships. It therefore becomes imperative for us as parents to set limits on our undertakings. Only by doing so can we have emotional reserves for our families. Learning how to protect family life and gaining confidence in the wisdom of this practice are important growing-up steps for us as parents.

Only recently have I learned about setting real limits on myself. We had five birthdays and two big trips in a three-month period this summer, and it was too much. Upon our return, we had gotten out of touch with each other, anger was floating around, and everyone was tired and irritable. It took us several days of enforced family time, many conversations, and much conscious loving to get back to normal. We might have avoided all this by knowing more accurately what our capacity is as a family.

Seeing the long-term effects of overload on families, you realize how necessary it is to take a long, critical look at that "just one more" volunteer project, client, coaching event, or activity for the children. You learn that what you put off today can be picked up later, at a better and less busy time for the family, and that when unexpected and uncontrollable busyness happens, you are better able to cope with it as a family if you have developed skills for "getting back to normal" and if you have not depleted yourselves by too many regular commitments.

It is proper for the caring family to protect its members, to protect its own ecosystem. The early years of the family are when values are established and defined, and during this time you will often feel the pull of the world "out there" as a threat to family life. It is not overprotective to establish strong family ties and values in the hearts of the children before they become a more active part of that world.

The young ones are fragile. Their communication and conflict-resolving skills are not finely honed. They do not understand the causes and effects of overstimulation. We as parents need to know it is important to limit our children's playtime, because we know that too much time spent without coming back to center—through quiet time alone or with the family— can result in an overtired and hyperactive child who then becomes more susceptible to illness. Dietary limitations, movie and television limitations, and social limitations are not out of line in the early years when family values are evolving. It is the family values, after all, that form the foundation for discipline in the home. If we choose not to spank, threaten, or coerce our children, then we must teach our values through *living example,* by preserving the family time needed to make open and spontaneous communication possible.

To preserve our family time, we need to protect ourselves as parents. We need to pamper ourselves, love ourselves, and praise ourselves for doing a good job. We need to protect ourselves from those who criticize our parenting and undermine our confidence. We need to seek out people, organizations, and books that uplift us and help us feel good about ourselves and about living in a family. We need to learn to plan and organize our time so that we have "people time" left over, and encourage everyone in the home to take personal responsibility so that one member does not become the family servant. And we need to spend time with one another in relaxed and unhurried ways. We may even need to schedule this time, to plan family retreats or soul-days and to reserve these occasions as we would any other important appointment to be kept.

We can gain the confidence to say no to some things. We can set limits that will empower us. We can encourage our children to treat one another with love and gentleness, and honor their family bond. It is important to cherish the family relationships that we have. It is always good for a family to have a sense of shared purpose. Growing good families helps everyone.

Talking with Children

When I think of myself as a child, I realize that my feelings were the same then as they are now. I am more graceful now, better at identifying and realizing my desires, more self-aware. But my heart and soul are the same. I am a continuum of one personality with ongoing refinements.

With this in mind, it becomes evident that my children are now building their own memories for their futures. I want those memories to be happy ones. Sometimes I try too hard for that. Sometimes I want to protect them from hurt and disappointment. When I realize that I can't and that I really don't want to deny them the full range of emotional experiences, I am able to let go of the feeling of total responsibility that one so easily feels as a parent.

It seems sometimes that everything our children do is a reflection of us. We see our behaviors in them. We know they get angry and grumpy when we are feeling out of sorts. And we can get angry when we see in our children behaviors that we are not comfortable with in ourselves. Our children touch us in such deep and sensitive places, and our anger at them is often a reflection of our own unresolved anger.

It's important to remember this association in the everyday scene of things, when chores and other responsibilities can lead to impatience and rote commands in our conflict intervention with our children. We look for surefire solutions to the discipline question. We so desperately want easy answers, want the conflict to go away. But how do we resolve conflicts with our children in a way that respects their personhood and remembers our own childhoods? This can seem like an impossible dilemma if our childhoods were not loving ones or if we feel we do not have the necessary tools for resolving conflicts with our loved ones in a new way.

Discipline techniques can come and go. We can "dare to discipline" and be "effectively trained" to enact some parenting scenario with our children, but it all boils down to talking to children, to loving them and to loving ourselves. And it helps to accept that we as parents are growing right along with our children, and are learning to *be* parents as each new challenge presents itself and as the children pass through each new phase. We are entitled to a few errors and will of necessity experience much anxiety.

As adults in the relationship, however, we cannot abdicate the decision-making responsibility that experience has given us. We have to get comfortable with making the hard decisions, saying the nos, setting the limits that our family is comfortable with. We have to become adults at precisely the time when we may feel the most helpless and overlooked. Aspiring to find a solution, a loving way to communicate with our children, is often enough. Aspiration in itself will do much to attract those ideas and philosophies and values we can learn from and model.

A few ideas can also help. In any conflict situation, as well as in day-to-day life, we can learn to talk to our children. This means listening and accepting exactly what they say about the way they feel in a particular situation, rather than trying to manipulate their perceptions to match our own. This means resisting the temptation to enter the discussion with a preconceived notion of what the solution should be, or to assume we have superior understanding simply because we are the adults. Rather, we have to seek a solution that takes our children's feelings into account, and we have to encourage our children to express their feelings to us by sharing ours with them.

We have to stop often to remember the child's emotional and

intellectual development. A child is in the process of becoming a person, of truly creating and developing his or her personhood through the experiences of childhood. And children often need detailed explanations of a situation and all its ramifications—not in a blaming way, but in a purely informative way. Remember, your child *wants* to reach a peaceful solution to conflicts, but does not always have the skills to express feelings or the occasions to do so in a supportive and nonthreatening environment.

Children are afraid of losing our love, just as we are afraid of losing the love of those important to us. We all want and need approval every day of our lives, simply by virtue of living in society and defining ourselves through our relationships with others. We need not to lose touch with our love for our children. We must not fall prey to the voices that hate children and see them as manipulative, selfish beings with no minds or feelings of their own.

And I suppose that we must at last let go of our desire for an easy 1-2-3 solution, a black-and-white outline for a personal drama that is dynamic and always on the verge of change. Raising children is one of those big, gray, learn-as-you-go areas. And here, we are best able to keep sight of one another and live in peaceful and pleasant coexistence by remembering to spend time together, to talk together, ask questions, air feelings, fears, hopes, and dreams; and by maintaining a simple trust in the lovability of ourselves and our children, and in our ability to manifest that love in our lives. However difficult this may be, it is worth the effort. For in striving comes personal transformation and hope for the future. What better future can we work for than the one created by meeting the ongoing challenges of daily life?

Expectations of Intimacy

W hen a subject beyond dispute first begins to be seriously questioned, we often see people polarizing over the issues. One side does not acknowledge the concerns of the other, but rather counters fear with fear in a neverending death litany. Our children will die if we immunize them; they will die if we don't. Homebirth risks the lives of babies; hospitals kill babies.

So, too, with carseats and working mothers. We are told that if we do not buckle up our babies, we risk their lives. We are told that if we work and leave our babies, we are risking their emotional futures, but if we stay home with them, we are risking our own. When we polarize over an issue, we rely on the emotional climate of fear rather than developing the logical and reasonable arguments that can support our intuition. And when we fail to acknowledge genuine concerns and fail to seek creative solutions to the problems that polarize us, we repress the full expression of our human potential.

One of the components of full human potential is the capacity for intimacy. We see that those people who inspire us have a great capacity for intimacy. Human beings learn by imitation and modeling, and just as young children learn the physical foundation for walking and talking, so too do they lay the emotional foundation for intimate behavior and relationship. Evidence is overwhelming from Sigmund Freud, John Bowlby, Jane Goodall, Selma Fraiberg, Arthur Janov, Ashley Montagu, and others that the early years are the most impressionable.

From this standpoint, it is curious that we make decisions

about our children's well-being as we do. We almost never treat them as social equals. We rarely consider their point of view as important as our own. We seldom treat our young children with the kind of active listening and common courtesy that we afford our adult friends. We know by our child's ability to communicate nonverbally that she or he has a point of view, but we often interpret it to support our own needs or fears.

Carseats and working mothers are cases in point. Only after we begin to talk to one another about carseats, do we realize the options between no carseats at all and keeping children strapped in carseats while they cry. We cannot begin to comprehend how a child perceives the experience of a carseat; and yet we know that he or she has no notion of the protection it is said to offer. It's tragic that in reaction to a fatal accident involving a drunk and an infant, our solution is to put infants in carseats rather than putting drunks in jail or taking away their licenses. When we polarize over the carseat issue, we fail to consider lowering speed limits, improving road conditions, mandating safety devices in cars, increasing penalties for drunk drivers, and other remedial measures. We also fail to look at the ways we can temporarily change our lives to accommodate a young child's needs while traveling.

When we polarize over the working mother issue, we hurt ourselves even more, creating a divide in a society where mothers need one another's support. We forget that the issue is not working or self-fulfillment. Women have always worked. They have picked roots and berries, they have harvested cotton, they have sweated in rice paddies, they have written books and painted masterpieces. The issue is not work. The issue is separation and how separation affects a person's relationship—especially how separation affects a baby's developing expectations of intimacy.

When we meet adults who don't want to "get involved" or don't want to "commit" themselves emotionally, we wonder what in that person's background contributed to this inability to form relationships. So, too, in the early years, we ask what kinds of life experiences best preserve the ability to form relationships, to love, and to grow.

If we fail to see that separation is the real problem among working mothers, then we will not look for the creative solutions beyond "quality daycare." We will not look at restructuring the marketplace to reflect our current awareness. Our ways of working are reminscent of the days when father was away from home for long hours while mother raised the children. Because we no longer accept this kind of family separation as ideal for any of its members, we need to do more to restructure our notions of *how* work is done, *where* it is done, and *how its worth is defined.*

If we polarize over the working mother issue, we fail to examine such solutions as working at home, recognizing mothering as real work, job sharing, guaranteed annual incomes for mothers, tax benefits for children, extended maternity and paternity leave, children in the marketplace, flexible hours, encouraging merchants to provide bathrooms for young children and changing rooms for babies, and striving for the acceptability of breastfeeding and the presence of children in public.

It's curious that we isolate the weakest members of our society. We put our young in daycare centers; we put our old in nursing homes; we put our emotionally compromised in prison. We continue to separate ourselves from those we love and from those we can't understand. I believe that we have the courage to face the difficulties of our relationships, and that until we are willing to acknowledge the needs of our loved ones along with our own, we will not realize our full human potential for intimacy.

Look How Far We've Come

As I begin to write, we are being hit with an unseasonable snowstorm. Unusual climatic occurrences such as these start one thinking of the worst. Certainly, we theorize, these weather changes are just further evidence that the temperature of the earth is shifting, that the ozone layer is thinning out, that the end of the world is coming.

Doom thinking, as I like to call it, is not new. I was recently reading the James Thurber story "Get Ready Man," about a man who 70 years ago rode around Columbus, Ohio, in a red convertible, bellowing, "Get Ready! Get Ready-y! The World Is Coming to an End!" Twenty years ago, when I went "back to the land," my move was fueled in part by a desire to be ready for the terrible future that awaited our world. Writings from the 19th century and earlier attest to the fact that dire forecasts of the future are both foolish and self-destructive.

My concern is that doom thinking creates the reality it predicts. Economic depression is certainly an extension of mental depression—of the people's loss of hope and their pessimism about the future. I believe that if we choose to think the end is coming, it may. If we choose to believe things are getting better, they will, because our openness to hope will help us find ways to change things and make them better.

So, I want to make a radical proposition. I want to say that this is the best time in history to be alive and that we have only increased wonder and happiness to look forward to. I say this not only because I look at the world through rose-colored glasses (I do), but because I see the fruit of the work of the last 30 years. I see that we have begun to move toward the solution of the big issues that face civilization today. And once we have begun, it is only a matter of time until they are solved.

My old friend Stephanie recently reminded me of how far we've come. She remarked on how different things are for our children than they were for us. Thirty years ago, racial integration was just beginning to become a public issue; today, people of all races mix freely, marry, and associate as equals in the business world. Thirty years ago, Martin Luther King was sitting in the back of the bus; today, a black man is a serious contender for president of the United States.

Thirty years ago, one didn't wear green and blue together, our skirts had to cover our knees, and long hair on men was un-American. Today, all kinds of color combinations and styles are acceptable, dress for men and women is more casual and less restrictive, school dress codes are a thing of the past, and men in ponytails and suits are common on city streets.

Thirty years ago, few people realized the connection between diet and disease. Today, natural food restaurants thrive everywhere.

Thirty years ago, disarmament was a topic for high school debates. We talked over cups of spearmint tea about what would happen if peace became popular. This issue has today reached public awareness, so much so that applications for new power plants are being rejected and people frequently line the streets to protest nuclear weapons. There is no way that the worldwide tide of nuclear disarmament can be turned back.

Fifteen years ago, we were happy if our husbands could be in the delivery room, and homebirths were secretive affairs that you kept from your obstetrician in hopes that your friend, a fledgling midwife, would know how to handle everything. Today, the move to legalize midwifery and the homebirth option is gaining momentum, and the force of the opposition indicates that this is indeed a serious wave of the future backed by increasing numbers of people all over the world.

Ten years ago, we had to advertise to attract people to the

first series meeting of La Leche League, "Why Breastfeed Your Baby?" Today, the majority of women at least *begin* breastfeeding, and it is common knowledge that breastmilk is the ideal food for babies.

Natural fiber clothing and wooden toys were hard to come by 17 years ago, when my first child was born. Today, there are so many manufacturers of these products that they are found in major department stores and children's stores and form a major part of mainstream marketing.

World hunger has come to the forefront as well. We are realizing that we can all be fed, that there is plenty in this world, and that some of us do not have to starve while the others feast. Young people are risking their lives in the open sea while dodging harpoons and saving whales. We are developing a conscience as a people. The ideas of the sixties have not died; they have taken root in personal action and commitment.

Twenty years ago, Lake Erie was dead. Today, it is alive and well and living in Buffalo, New York.

Another sign that our ideas have come of age is that we are able to laugh at ourselves. Once we are able to laugh at ourselves, we know that our ideas have become so much a part of us that they can no longer be threatened.

So, I contend again that this is the best time to be alive. We may experience shakiness and fear as we move more fully into this renaissance, but such emotions only signify that we have shed one skin to grow another. We must focus on a positive future if we are to create it.

We must accept the fact that we re-create the world daily by what we think. We must take responsibility for seeing how far we've come, and for celebrating and applauding ourselves as we move forward with the changes still to be made. Our lives will always be in a state of creative flux if we are committed to living them with personal responsibility and concern for our fellow human being. There is always more to be done, but look at how far we've come!

Experts in Silence

In the past year, the marriages of several of my closest friends have broken up. These were "long" marriages—7 years, 9 years, and 15 years. The breakups shook me to the core. These were families with whom I had commiserated about the divorces all around us. These were the parents of my children's friends.

While it is sometimes obvious why this or that couple has problems or differences, one always wonders what went wrong. Certainly, these partners loved each other once. What made them stop loving or stop trying to love or stop trusting enough to see their way back to love? In each of these relationships, and in many others, one thing that happened was silence. Secrets were kept; certain subjects became taboo; some topics became too personally threatening.

I heard a man and a woman talking in a store the other day. They had each just broken up with a partner and were looking forward to living alone again. Each one had been smothered in the relationship and felt that relationships in general were hopeless, bound to enslave, and much too difficult to sustain. I chuckled throughout most of their conversation. The most obvious thing about relationships is that they are not easy. Nor does being with the"right" person eliminate the problems that may arise. *Every* relationship requires care and attention in order to be sustained. Even though some relationships may appear drought resistant or weatherproof, these qualities do not "just happen." I, too, have foolishly hoped that relationships would just work themselves out with good intentions, but I have learned that no two people can have a serious relationship of any kind without some disagreement between them.

How do we resolve these inevitable differences? We may decide it is the other person's fault and dismiss the situation. We may resort to silence, to punishment through avoidance, to refusing eye contact, or to not initiating conversation about an uncomfortable issue or about anything really substantial. We may hang on to anger, to personal judgments about who is right and who is wrong. Or we may seek resolution. We can commit ourselves to not letting bad feelings go too long or involve too many people. We can deal directly with things and with people. We can risk anger with others, especially our partner.

My husband and I have just learned how to fight with each other. Until recently, we were too afraid to fight, too fearful of hurt. We learned as our marriage progressed that we were not immune to conflicts, and we saw aspects of each other that hadn't changed and that would have to be addressed. We got tired of our patterns of silence, of approach and withdrawal, of separation by anger. By risking anger with each other, we are becoming more honest.

People are so often afraid to be honest. We diffuse our anger over a situation by griping to a friend about it. We rarely just stop in our tracks and comment on our immediate reaction to a statement or an incident. And yet, it is possible to direct this kind of information in a nonaccusatory way and to have a conflict encounter that will help a relationship grow. When feelings toward someone are not directed to that person but are dumped on someone else, or are left free to pollute the psychic atmosphere that we all share, the effects are far-reaching. Feelings are real. Do not be fooled by the fact that they are not visible. Emotions have power and must go somewhere. If feelings are not responded to directly, they build walls between people, they cause illness—they create physical and emotional pain. If I do not deal immediately with the person involved in my emotion, I begin to project that emotion onto those around

me. I get angry at the kids when I am really angry at the person
I just spoke with on the phone. I start to see fault in everything.
I start to have negative feelings about myself. However, if I go
directly and tell the person I feel angry or confused, we may
have a little fight and clear the air, but we will feel better
toward one another afterwards.

Even those of us in the habit of expressing our feelings
directly will sometimes sit on a situation and mull it over.
Occasionally a feeling will pass or be resolved in our minds.
When feelings don't pass, when they continue to raise anger
every time they are discussed, then they need to be dealt with
and put to rest. Holding on to them holds up everything else.

Working together on a magazine offers wonderful opportunities for learning how to resolve conflict. The many changes at
our office, the new staff and new machinery, have left us wondering if anything would ever be the same again. Some have
reacted to change by holding on to an incident or emotion. It
begins in the air as a charged and suspicious feeling. There can
be mutterings, innuendos, avoidance—all unnecessary uses of
energy. Emotions must be expressed more spontaneously.
Loving others, we work toward their spiritual evolution as well
as our own, and we need candor and honesty to ensure this
evolution.

Depression is anger turned inward. If we are angry and cannot say so or respond spontaneously with emotion, we turn this
anger inward and rationalize our fear of dealing with it. In our
easy silence, we begin to hate ourselves because we are left
alone with the demons inside our own minds.

We are experts in silence, in avoiding, snubbing, and being
good little girls and boys at the expense of our emotions. We
may not overcome the fear of expressing anger by giving vent
to it; but with practice, we can learn how to express our anger
more gracefully. Every time we risk anger, we open to the possibility that someone will confirm our worst fears about ourselves. But we are so much more than we imagine, so much

more than we give ourselves credit for. Always capable of being more, we grow just by reaching out to others. Even if we bungle, we are strong for having done so.

We can reach out of our silence by remembering our infinite capacity for change and for personal evolution. We also have an infinite capacity for love. The more we give, the more we have to give. Our lives and the lives of our children can all benefit as we meet the challenges in our relationships with risk, honesty, and present-tense love expressed through spontaneous emotion. We can learn to fail in silence.

Conscious Parenting: Keeping the Light Shining

Many of us seek consciousness through spiritual and religious teachings. Sometimes we think our spiritual goal is to be perfect. Sometimes we believe nirvana or heaven is just around the corner. Day-to-day situations, however, seem to challenge our spiritual truths and cause us to fall short of ideals of perfection by reacting with *real* human emotions. We feel we fail when we experience the strong emotions of parenthood. Indeed, we have not failed. We have plunged into living. Our goal in this world is not to repress our human emotions, but to experience them. Our goal in this world is not to be spiritual, and certainly not to be perfect. Our goal is to be conscious.

It is our work as humans to be *in the world* and to experience its joys *and* its sorrows. By staying conscious in the world, especially in the world of parenthood, we can develop a central focus, a personal witness to our lives. Being conscious as a parent, however, does not mean that we have it all figured out or that we escape problems. It means that by paying attention to what we do as parents, by taking our parenting work seriously, and by learning to observe situations with mental, emotional, and spiritual honesty, we develop the ability to respond meaningfully to our children.

We are conscious of what we do as parents because, as parents, we are the real experts regarding our children. The answers about how to parent don't exist outside of ourselves. Sometimes we don't have an answer, but this doesn't mean that someone else does or that a delay in understanding is abnormal. In fact, such delays become opportunities to observe ourselves and our children, to ask others to share their experiences, or to do some reading and develop a perspective that may, in the end, only serve to confirm what we already know.

Being a conscious parent means learning how to stir up those good feelings that keep us inspired and learning how to maintain them. Those good feelings intensify when we understand the importance of our work as parents. We have the opportunity to grow as our children grow, and staying open to this opportunity helps us stay open to the changing needs of our children. It's important to give ourselves permission to be around people who inspire us, to choose friends who support our parenting beliefs, and to avoid situations in which we feel attacked as a parent.

To be a good parent, to be good at loving, it is also important to be good and loving to ourselves. We need quiet time, recreation, relaxation, laughter, good company, and food for the soul. These forms of nourishment do much to rejuvenate family members.

My family enjoyed a long, wonderful vacation this past summer. There was lots of stimulation and many special moments with exciting people. We secretly imagined that we had really reached "perfect happiness" this time. We were able to stay conscious of our goals as a family, and to remember why we wanted the good feelings to abound: to feel free to be who we are, to feel free to express our feelings without attack, and to learn how to stay in the present.

After returning from this wonderful, uplifting vacation, I felt discouraged. The day-to-day routines and responsibilities seemed to distract from the good centered feelings I had enjoyed so much. Then I realized that the challenge for us as parents is to keep the flame of love alive for our children and for the world. When our light burns brightly, it kindles many candles. We all serve one another.

Part of the work of keeping this flame of love alive is focusing on a creative and concrete vision for our family rather than merely reacting to what is around us. How different, for example, to hope for peace, to expect peace, rather than to fear nuclear disaster. How different to remain open to the cooperation of our "problem child" rather than labeling this child forever uncooperative. Observing current realities, we can make a new vision for the family, and take action to move in that direction. By setting visions for family life, we open ourselves up to an entire organic process that will work to materialize these visions.

Much can be changed by conscious focus. Neurological research reveals a link between the seat of consciousness in the brain and the origin of consciousness in the heart. The workings of the heart interact with the workings of the brain. And quantum physics underscores religious and philosophical teachings by observing that a person's awareness of something can change its reality. Waves become particles simply by being observed. Consciousness creates form from energy.

We have unlimited power for creating positive change, for leading productive and happy lives, and for helping others. It all begins at home, as a commitment to loving ourselves by recognizing ourselves as experts with our children and by trusting ourselves to learn how to parent. Keeping the light of love alive in our hearts, in our interactions with our families, and in our reaching out to others, we spread the light around. Only when we all get it will we be free.

A Vision for the Future

The October 4–6, 1985, edition of *USA Today* carried a story of the peace initiatives that Soviet leader Mikhail Gorbachev made to France and Britain. In response to the seriousness of purpose evidenced by the new and sophisticated Russian diplomat, President Ronald Reagan said, "It would be nice to hope they may have gotten religion." The Soviets say they want to reduce nuclear weapons, discontinue missile projects, stop Star Wars. Reagan says they need religion.

The old guard dies hard. The images of a vengeful god of fear and retaliation, blame and guilt, are on their way out, but they are dying hard. We are coming of age. Our generation throughout the world, singing for hunger, marching for peace, is coming of age. And we no longer fear the Russians. We know they are not coming for us in the night. We don't have to immunize ourselves against them. We know our bodies and our souls can handle a world society.

The old guard still lives in fear. The old guard sees black and white, good and bad. The old guard has given up responsibility for the world. We, however, are learning how to claim that responsibility, how to use it consciously, how to clean up the world. We know that we are in charge, that we are the world, that we are the people.

My friends, it's only a matter of time. Be patient. Do not be afraid. The dark will rise further before it stumbles, groans, and topples. We can handle that too. We can wait. We know that all aspects of the process must come to fruition. What will be, after the waiting, will be glorious.

What we do now in our own homes, in our own ways paves the way for the future. Our work now is to create the new vision for the future. We love one another, and we don't stop trying when we fail. We work to transform anger, fear, and violence in our lives. We learn to love Russians. The great Fyodor Dostoyevsky said, "Until you have become really, in actual fact, a brother to everyone, brotherhood will not come to pass." We can teach our children to think of themselves as world citizens. We can teach them to embrace cooperation along with competition. We don't have to lie to them anymore. We don't have to tell them that playing the game is as much fun as winning; they clearly see that winning is what people get excited about. We can learn, along with our children, alternatives to self-definition through winning, comparing, and basing one's sense of self-worth on another. In dropping this perception of comparative worth, we also release our propensity to find a wrongdoer for every wrong, to blame others for our own bad feelings, and to buy violence in thought, if not in action.

Imagine with me for a while. . . . Imagine what the future could be like. Replace the dour, depressed images of doom with an uplifting picture. Help to create a wonderful future by your own mental contributions to it. Can you see it now? Can you see it rolling? Won't it be nice when we all live together in peace?

There will be Russian films, Russian food, Russian dance, Russian fashions, Russian humor and pathos. In the process of learning how to love other countries, we will learn how to love one another and ourselves. We will have had to.

We will have had to learn to love children again, too. Won't it be nice when every store you enter has a bathroom for children, a play table with crayons and books, and a comfortable chair for a nursing mom? Won't it be nice when everyone you meet gives you just the right advice about breastfeeding, childbirth, and childrearing? Won't it be nice when every conversation you have about birth helps you feel comfortable rather than afraid, when real fears are confronted and unnecessary ones are not conjured up?

Won't it be nice when your baby comes and everyone in your neighborhood or circle of friends brings meals each day for weeks, cleans up your house a bit, and sees that you have a diaper service? Won't it be nice when others eagerly help you comfort your child, rather than encourage you to keep the little one quiet through repression, bribery, or violence? Won't it be nice when we grant ourselves permission to defend our children—and our own intuitions—in social, educational, and medical settings?

Won't it be nice to love teenagers again? Won't it be nice when every town has a teen center where teens can go, be safe, and have fun during their period of exploration? Won't it be nice when old people are honored, respected, learned from, and not feared? Won't it be nice when we again know the humor of human frailty, the brief time given to explore it, and the purpose of transcending its boundaries through loving?

In expanding our consciousness, what will we have? We will have a global society—one that loves children, nurtures and cherishes its elders, and offers protection and possibility to all beings. We will then see the human experience with true understanding and participate in the evolution of planetary consciousness.

What is this mind we have? What are these emotions? Are there any limits to human potential? Can we calm the world so that we can begin the inner journeys? Won't it be nice when we all live together in peace? What is your vision for the future?

Plunge into Parenting

It is not the easy issues of parenting that consume us, not the baby clothes or the bathing techniques or the color of the nursery. While these issues may become a receptacle for our fears, it is the questions regarding our own personal competence and survival as parents that really concern us. The details get worked out in the process, but the story of our personal transformations through parenting is what longs to be told.

What parenting touches in us is the inner life that it feeds and transforms. Having children can be a tremendous opportunity to learn about oneself and others and to learn better ways of loving. This learning is accomplished by plunging into parenting, by pushing beyond our personal, intellectual, and emotional limitations again and again. As a teenager swimming competitively, I learned that I could reach the finish even when I could no longer feel my legs. As a parent, I have learned that I can keep my ideals of parenting intact by pushing beyond what I think I am capable of.

The advantage of plunging into parenting rather than recoiling from its demands is that through plunging one learns what is on the other side of fear, what is on the other side of confusion in the night, what is on the other side of limitation and resistance. By facing and plunging into an experience of parenting that tests us, we demonstrate to ourselves that we are equal to that experience and that we can, in fact, transform the experience into something that serves us rather than defeats us. Transforming the challenges of parenting, overcoming the difficulties in a way that meets our ideals, teaches us that we can learn something new, again and again.

The primary way that we can learn to go beyond our limits in parenting is to trust our child. There is a danger in overintellectualizing the parenting experience. Books, tapes, and videos proliferate, each one promising the secret to perfect parenting, each one seeking to encapsulate the human experience in a few hundred pages. It is impossible to sort out all of this information without coming back time and time again to our child. Look to your child. Ideas are only ideas; opinions are culturally dictated. Your child, however, is new, uncluttered, without any of the learned trappings of modern civilization or the dichotomies of intellectual reasoning. Your child's needs and wants are identical. He or she is programmed by nature to learn not through behavior modifications, but through seeking the matrix, the mother. Your child does not recognize the nature of his or her discomfort, whether it is from fatigue or hunger or just plain loneliness, but instinctually seeks solace from the one who can identify and alleviate the discomfort. Some contemporary childrearing techniques undermine this type of instinctual system and end up teaching the child that his or her needs will not be met. Methods cannot teach the child not to need.

Implicit in trusting your child is trusting yourself. I believe in an implicit destiny in the order of things, whereby each child on some level chooses his or her parents. If this is so, then it must also be so that each child's parents will make the best choices for that child. Ask yourself what kinds of experiences, readings, and relationships help you get in touch with yourself, and trust your innate capacity to accomplish what you desire. Protect yourself from opinions and advice that undermine your confidence, and surround yourself with ideas and people who inspire your best parenting aspirations.

We human beings are so resilient that we can barely imagine our potential. We are so wonderful, so willing to be happy, to be kind, to start over. Just think of how much potential there is in the human soul for an individual to be truly self-regulated, to grow up totally trusted and self-trusting from the very beginning of life. Think of how confident such a person could be, how much he or she could learn with this sort of confidence inside—true confidence, not born of courage or learned through experience, but always present, honored, and intact from the moment of birth. A human being could live without fear if fear were not created for him or her in the first place.

To learn to trust yourself and your child means learning to surrender to the experience of parenting and learning how futile it is to try to control what is happening. We all experience panic periods in parenting, times when we wonder what we've gotten ourselves in for. Maybe this panic period concerns waking in the night, or wondering how to talk to a child who is no longer a baby, or doubting our capacity to parent a teen. Whatever the cause of the panic is, whenever the fear comes ripping in, we must let go and allow it to be until it is clear what to do, until we have integrated the new learning that is required by the new experience so that we will, on the other side, have a clearer understanding of a comfortable course of action or attitude. We learn by plunging in again and again, trusting ourselves to figure it all out because we have done so before.

To surrender to the experience of parenting, it is important to learn to live in the present moment. This lesson begins at the beginning with the new baby who nurses "all the time." If you plunge into parenting, you sit—impatiently at first—in the rocking chair, watching the dust pile up on the rug until you finally learn to relax and let it go, until you finally learn to mother. You discover that you *will* get it done, that you will be worrying about the same old dust long after your baby is grown, and that you can be faster and more efficient because the plunging in teaches you how to get more done in less time. If you succumb to the fear, if you put the baby down before he or she is finished, or let the baby cry awhile so that you can do just one more thing, you will only remain at the same level of depth.

Plunge into parenting. Let go of your misconceptions, pre-conceptions, and fears about how things should be, how you imagine that they might turn out, and simply respond to your child moment by moment with full trust in his or her inherent goodness. Your first response should be to trust that your child has a good reason for his or her behavior and to further trust that you can figure out what it is. Ask yourself how conflicts with your child really serve you, what you learn from them, and why you react the way you do.

Children are, after all, our mirrors. They play back to us what they have learned from us. While at times this may seem unbearable, in the bearing and the looking, we learn that we can go beyond our self-imposed limitations and reap rich rewards in learning that we *can* learn, *can* change, *can* adapt and face new panic periods of parenting with true confidence rather than mustered courage. A child strips away our illusions that we are perfect, that we have it all figured out, that we are all grown up. In fact, we grow up with our children if we are willing to remain open to their innate goodness as well as our own.

An Inner Mother

An illustration from a calendar my friend Mary gave me depicts the face of a child. And pictured within the mind of the child is the likeness of his mother. What this illustration says to me is that the mother lives within the mind of the child. We all know this, really. We realize that most of what our children learn, they learn from modeling—from what they see acted out around them. In the last few decades, parents have become increasingly aware that what they do as parents may be the most important work they will do. How can we act on this awareness, however, without taking ourselves so seriously that we lose all spontaneity as parents, or lose trust in our innate instincts to parent, or let the intellect overrule the heart in responding to our children?

It is all a matter of balance. A mother is always balancing, always wondering when to step in, when to step back. She is always aware of the changes in her relationship with her child, of the changes in her child's development, and of the corresponding changes in her responses to her child. Mother is the giver; child is the taker; and yet, the mother must sometimes model the taker role so the child learns the reality of personal limitations. What was appropriate and felt good at one stage of a child's life, begins to feel oppressive or too demanding in another. We pull back, we experience resistance, and finally we set a new pattern. Then a new habit of relating develops. We grow with our children when we appreciate our own growth.

Balancing our own growth with our child's needs involves trusting. It involves trusting the heart more than the head. And it involves seeing all changes as helpful. While we may not have the vision to see the whole picture, we know there is a bigger picture. This may be one of our first lessons as parents. We don't know what lies ahead, nor do we know the reasons for our experiences—the good or the bad—so our best choice is to trust. In the words of *Starseed Transmissions*, "Hope for nothing but what is, and see its fullness in every moment."

Because we don't know the whole story, we may sometimes wonder what degree of involvement is necessary to be a mother. Is the mother of a child with high needs or with disabilities *more* of a mother than the mother of an "easygoing" child? Is the mother of a large family more of a mother than the mother of one? Is someone who can articulate her mothering experience and inspire others with it more of a mother than one who does not find her mothering inspirational? Is any parent-child relationship easy? I think not. There is always a new challenge around the corner.

A mother meets these new challenges and learns to be a mother through listening to her heart, through developing an inner agreement with truth that allows ready recognition. But how does she learn to hear her heart amid all the "experts" and those who say, "My baby slept through the night from day one"or "You'll spoil him."? How does one sort out the truly helpful from the patronizing? How does a mother hear herself through all of this?

Some beliefs that bring me back to center about my relationship with my children are again based on trust. I believe that a baby's wants and needs are the same. That a baby does not manipulate. That a baby seeks the matrix, the mother, so the mother can solve the problems that arise. If a baby needs something—cuddling, nursing, holding—the baby seeks the mother who can *respond* to the baby even if she doesn't always understand the cause of distress. We often wonder when a baby's needs and wants stop being identical, and I'm not sure they ever do. Behind my children's incomprehensible or less tolerable behaviors is usually a simple misunderstanding, not an attempt to manipulate. Seeing into the heart of a behavior, I can often discover the real need; and once this is acknowledged, the behavior changes on its own.

Other beliefs that help sustain my relationship with my children are the sense that the child is perfect and doing the best he or she can at any given moment and the sense that the parent is perfect and doing his or her best at any given moment. At a parenting workshop recently, I listed these beliefs on a blackboard and, upon returning from a break, found that "The parent is perfect" had been erased. We surely are hard on ourselves, imagining that perfection comes only in trying harder, in avoiding all mistakes, all unexpected changes, all pain and discomfort. But there is no place for blame, guilt, and fear in our relationship with our children—or in our view of ourselves as parents. We are all doing our best at every given moment. Why, on earth, would we do less?

Acknowledging that child and parent are perfect and are in a holy relationship, you gain the inner conviction that you, as parent, have the answer. When you are confused about your relationship with your child, when you are taking too much responsibility for it all and feeling guilty and hopeless about things ever getting better, you do not need a solution. No one can give you that. What you need is the stillness and confidence and quiet of your mind and soul so that you can *hear* the answer. For the answer is within. The mind that asks the question supplies the answer; and even if the answer has been floating around for centuries, it is a new answer every time someone new hears it. Who else but the parent really knows the child, really has all the information needed for the fullest answer?

You and your child form the hub of a great wheel from which spokes go in and out in all directions to the world. Find your way back to the center of that wheel, whatever your way may be. Realize how important your job is as a parent. And understand that to nurture and love others with the grace you desire means taking care of yourself and cultivating your own inner harmony. Inner harmony grows not by finding ways to get away from your child, but by giving yourself the gift of a hot bath at the end of a long day, reading a book of poetry, talking to a friend on the phone, taking a nap, crying, getting a massage, having a day off from cleaning and cooking, staying in your pajamas all day, swimming, going out to eat, or attending a conference. Do something for yourself as you give. Learn to laugh at yourself and not take yourself so seriously.

Learning to give to your child, you learn to give to yourself, to mother yourself. Then the circle, the wheel, the hub, mother and child go around and around and around, as they have for centuries, learning to love, learning to appreciate the fullness of each moment—light and heavy—learning to simply be.

Do We Need It All?

A popular women's magazine recently published a feature on women who "have it all": baby, exciting marriage, and flourishing career. Dozens of full-color photographs showed famous women and their children. Captions pointed out that these women did not let their children interfere with their careers. The underlying assumption of the feature was that women could have it all if they did not let their emotional commitments stand in the way of their careers.

It is a curious logic that we embrace. It assumes that to achieve worth in our society, one must not let emotional commitments—the people one loves—stand in the way of material pursuits. When women subscribe to this logic, they are following an outdated male model of professional achievement, a model that has not served us in the past and against which many of us still rebel.

The male model of professional achievement played a starring role in our parents' generation. As a result, many of us today lament the fact that we didn't know our fathers, that they were often absent from home, that we had no idea what their work life was like. Fathers of that generation were encouraged to be breadwinners and leave childrearing to women. We have criticized the female counterpart to this scenario—women as family servants—while lusting after our absent daddies by imitating their obsession with the material world.

As children, it did not serve us to have parents who were physically or emotionally absent from the home. How can we integrate this awareness while still honoring our desires for

51

personal achievement and the necessity for making a living? It is not easy, but I believe that neither women nor men must realize their full potential at the expense of their relationships with those they love. On the contrary, it is often these very relationships that form the basis of the "inner" learning that is the real reason for human existence beyond any career in the "outer" world.

The balance between work and family life is always changing and requires frequent readjusting. During the intense years of early parenting, when children are under five and their physical needs are so great, a couple is challenged to stay in touch with one another. And when the intense physical needs are satisfied, the intense emotional needs of older children emerge. All of these events affect one's ability to focus on work or even *do* work outside the home. Observers of the workplace know that home life influences work performance. This important human domain must be preserved; we must insist that the definition of work change to acknowledge the reality of family life.

The United States is among the least progressive nations in terms of supporting the working parent. Some Scandinavian countries offer a nine-month paid leave for new parents. Maybe it's good that we have been slow to institute financial aid to parents, because the lack of assistance forces us to be innovative and to look for broader social solutions to employment and parent-child separation.

Women owe it to themselves to find solutions because it is the woman as mother who is stuck in the middle of this dilemma. Trying to be either the perfect mother or the perfect career woman or the perfect both, she is enslaved by a projection of herself. This projection does not allow her to easily surrender to the experiences of being a woman—experiences like pregnancy, birth, and mothering.

Birth and parenting are great transformative events, great life-changing and life-enhancing events. These are not accomplishments to be compared and measured. They impact on our past and our future, and constitute a test for us—one not to be overcome and conquered, but to be surrendered to. Modern woman, with all the negative connotations of the feminine in her psyche, may distrust or resist the surrender of birth. Pursuits in the outer world, pursuits that compete with her emotional commitments, and belief systems that view emotional commitments as second-rate can further undermine the ability to surrender.

An ability to surrender is a great asset for a new mother. It enables her to give herself permission to be mothered as she learns to mother. In our passion to distance ourselves from the helpless woman of the past who screams in childbirth, we chose instead to emulate the primitive woman who hops down from the horse to birth her baby, hops back on, and rides off to catch up with her tribe. We mistook what is possible for what is desirable.

In fact, birthing and postpartum women throughout the world commonly acknowledge a seclusion period immediately following the birth of the baby. Some societies include lengthy postpartum rituals. The new mother is pampered, taken care of, fed, kept warm, and nourished in such a way as to accent her transition from an introspective time of pregnancy and birth to a postpartum reunion with the outer world. While we believe that we do not need these rituals to ensure our physical survival, having respect and reverence for the fragility of the mother-infant dyad nourishes the emotional and spiritual strength of the new mother and eases her into the new responsibilities of parenthood.

Our ability to appreciate the richness of the emotional and personal side of life, to surrender to pregnancy and birth and postpartum, and to surrender to life in general is threatened by our obsession with having it all. We can only have it all by exerting the kind of control over our lives that excludes the possibility of the unexpected or mysterious. It is our loved ones, not our worldly accomplishments, that keep us warm in the night; and it is our children who keep us from taking ourselves too seriously. They help us to clarify our priorities, and remind us that people are more important than things and that being with people takes time.

The Nature of Dependency

I recently spoke to a friend who had her first baby six months ago. She told me that she was going to start her totally breastfed baby on a bottle so that she could get out more. What I really sensed was that she believed she had to teach her baby to be more independent, that perhaps his dependency was her fault. I realized that she shared the misconception common among new parents that independence is something that *can* be taught. Rather, independence is something that unfolds out of the nature of the child after he or she has had an opportunity to experience and outgrow dependency.

We have a cultural bias toward dependency, toward any emotion or behavior that indicates weakness, and this is nowhere more tragically evident than in the way we push our children beyond their inner limits and timetables. We establish outside standards as more important than inner experience when we wean our children rather than trusting that they will wean themselves; when we insist that our children sit at the table and finish their meals rather than trusting that they will eat well if healthful food is provided on a regular basis; and when we toilet train them at an early age rather than trusting that they will learn to use the toilet when they are ready. By assuming that we as parents know what is best for our children in regard to their inner experience, and that we must show them how and when to accomplish basic human developmental tasks, we teach them that outside standards are more important and more accurate indicators than signals from within themselves.

Two recent scientific studies reflect this cultural bias against weakness and dependency in children. One study compared children who were vaccinated while in their mothers' arms with children who were vaccinated without their mothers present. Those who were vaccinated in the absence of their mothers cried less, and thus the researchers concluded that it would be better for pediatricians to discourage the presence of mothers during vaccination because children appeared to handle the shots better without them. Obviously, the researchers in this study were biased against emotional expressiveness and believed that such expressiveness in children under stress was a weakness.

My experience is just the opposite. I have noticed that my four children are wonderful when we are on trips away from home. They handle things well, get along with one another, and accept irregular sleeping and eating experiences—only to come home and fall apart. Once at home, they fight, cry, and laze around. I believe it is normal for people of all ages to hold it together while facing a stressful situation and then to let down and fall apart, if necessary, once they are in a safe environment. For a child, this safe environment is home, mother, or father. It was perfectly normal for those vaccinated children to cry under the stress of the experience, and the presence of their mothers gave them the confidence to cry. The conclusion of this study might have been that it is better to vaccinate children with their mothers present so that the children can better handle the experience.

A study conducted by Margaret Burchinal of the University of North Carolina at Chapel Hill, and reported in the February 1987 issue of *Psychology Today*, compared young children raised at home by their mothers with young children who had attended daycare since infancy. This study concluded that children cared for away from home "appeared" less insecure than those cared for at home. While one might argue that assessing what "appears" to be insecurity is a subjective evaluation that does not belong in a scientific study, my experience tells me that insecurity is an appropriate response. Young children are especially sensitive to new people in their environment, and this sensitivity changes as their environment changes. Each of my children, for example, related to strangers differently, and this difference was directly connected with how many people outside the home we saw. My fourth child, who has been raised knowing the many people who work on the magazine, sometimes appears more secure as a youngster than did my first child, who was raised in a more isolated, rural environment.

Those who study animal behavior will tell you that baby animals, known for their curiosity, are even more cautious than curious. Is caution to be considered insecurity? It is as though we expect our children to arise fully socialized from the womb, and do not accept that their experiences with the world, their individual personalities, and the simple passage of time are what develop socialization. (This study has been further criticized for its biases and lack of correlational evidence.)

By rejecting the expressions of "weakness" in children— behaviors that we also reject in adults—we set children at war within themselves. For one thing, we establish an arbitrary standard of behavior that purports to dictate more about what is best for them than does their own inner experience. And for another, we pass along the habit of rejecting immediate responses in favor of intellectual rationale.

I have recently begun to learn acceptance of my children's "weaker" emotions. When my first child (now 12) was a baby, I would run to her and whisk her up each time she hurt herself. My exaggerated response taught her to believe that being hurt was a terrifying experience that she could not handle. My fourth child, on the other hand, is very noisy when she gets hurt. I don't run to her or overreact; I don't try to fix things. But she screams and carries on, and I have had to train myself to just let that be. By accepting her rich emotional response, and by treating her injury without showing excessive indifference, I have found that her "extreme" emotional reaction is usually shortlived. Fully experiencing her painful reality, she is free to leave it and move on to experience other realities in the moment.

Certainly, *some* checking of our inner impulses is needed to live as social beings. It is through this checking that we learn such socially acceptable behavior as using a toilet, eating with a spoon, and wearing clothing. But when this checking of the inner experience by the intellect becomes moralistic rather than practical, when it becomes too extreme, or when we continually teach our children to believe that we know what is best for them, we rob the child of the essential birthright of self-regulation.

The child who grows to adulthood lacking this sense of self-regulation and distrusting his or her own inner experience may become an adult victimized by addictions. When I look around me, I see most of us struggling in one way or another with compulsive behavior—overeating, overresponsibility, smoking cigarettes, taking recreational drugs, overworking, drinking alcohol or caffeine, seeking the guru—trying in some way to find perfection outside of ourselves or to distract ourselves from the endless striving for perfection. I believe that these compulsions and addictions have their origins in the seemingly well-intended repressions of childhood. A child who is taught to exercise control using external standards learns to set up an inner duality between what is immediately experienced and what is supposed to be, and learns to believe that there *is* a perfect way to be. The adult who lives with this duality finds distractions and diversions that provide respite from the overzealous striving for perfection, but the diversions that may have been harmless as a child can be dangerous as an adult.

Our job as parents is to understand and honor the nature of dependency in the child. Dependency, insecurity, and weakness are natural states for the child. They are natural states for all of us at times, but for children—especially young children—they are predominant conditions. And they are outgrown, just as we grow from crawling to walking, from babbling to talking, from puberty into sexuality. As humans, we move from weakness to strength. We move from uncertainty into mastery. When we refuse to acknowledge the stages prior to mastery, we teach our children to hate and distrust their weakness, and we start them on the journey of a lifetime to reintegrate their personalities.

I cannot stress enough the importance of trusting our children, trusting them in their entirety. Accepting their weaknesses as well as their strengths, their ugly emotions as well as their beautiful ones, their disasters as well as their triumphs, their dependency as well as their independence, is to give them the gift of a whole life. And as whole beings who are not at war within themselves, they will not be at war with others.

It is the nature of the child to be dependent, and it is the nature of dependence to be outgrown. Begrudging dependency because it is not independence is like begrudging winter because it is not yet spring. Dependency blossoms into independence in its own time.

The Push and Pull of Love

I often write about honoring the needs of the child and appreciating dependency in the child. And yet, we all wonder at times how meeting the needs of the child affects the needs of the parents, and if it is possible for children to be *too* dependent.

My tendency has been to do more for my last child than I have done for the other three simply because there has not been a new baby around to remind me of how capable she really is. So I have dusted off the distinction between needs and habits made by Dr. James Hymes in *The Child under Six*. Habits are fairly easily changed. If they are long-standing, the change may meet with resistance, but behavior does not regress. Needs, on the other hand, are not easy to change, and when they are not met, they become channeled into other behavior. When we try substituting, avoiding, delaying, and saying no, and nothing works, we probably have a need on our hands.

The balance between honoring dependence and encouraging independence is delicate. I am continually redefining this balance at every stage of parenting. How do I sympathize with my 11 year old's frustration with himself over hurting his brother again without condoning his behavior? How do I encourage my four year old to find her own shoes without giving her the impression that I don't want to help her? How do I encourage my eight year old to slow down without making him defensive? And how do I appreciate the growing pains and heightened sensitivity of my 12 year old while still insisting on peace in the family?

We know from observing others that it *is* possible to give too much, to take care of children in ways that disempower them, to be afraid to say no for fear that it will be experienced as not loving enough. Incapacitating our children in these ways prevents them from realizing their full potential, and we do this most often when we are overly anxious about them. Children are quite literally made from the life substance of the mother, and because of this vital connection, they are susceptible to her subtle fears and anxieties. It is therefore important to discipline our minds to free our children of parental anxieties and fears.

It is also important to share empowering information that helps move our children toward independence. When my children were younger, I was often confused about the age at which they "should" clean their rooms, do the dishes, or brush their teeth. I assumed that they would just *do* these things, and I didn't want to take responsibility for their behavior by constantly reminding them. Now I see that at the appropriate age, it was fairly easy to encourage them to do these things, while at an inappropriate age, it was nearly impossible. And I understand that it takes time for behaviors to become regular, just as it takes time to move from dependence to independence. During this time, I try to communicate my expectations to my children, to help them understand how their behavior fits in with the needs of the other family members, to teach them how to do the things I expect them to do, and to anticipate some backsliding.

Age appropriateness is also subject to change, and it is important to test the limits of behavior from time to time to see if they *have* changed. Just when you believe that your child may never clean her room, she may surprise you by doing it all by herself. Her unique readiness is augmented by the potentiality that you keep ever open in your mind. A parent can prolong dependence and contribute to a child's "bad" habits by holding a limited definition and expectation, one that may be hard for the child to overcome. Keep an open vision for your child.

Another way of prolonging dependence is by doing too

much for your child. In the early years, this may mean dressing and feeding children when they need to experiment with these skills on their own. Later, it may mean doing a child's chores because it's easier to do it your way, or refusing to set limits on a child's activities. Considering the myriad of activities that children are involved in today, a family can easily lose touch if they are going in too many different directions.

When my husband found himself spending too much time chauffeuring our children to various classes, we decided to cut back on some of their outside activities. The children greeted this decision at first with resistance and then with relief. For children who experiment with limits, parental definitions can be like a set of guardrails they can bounce off of, giving them some sense of limits in a world that often seems limitless. In a subtle way, doing too much for your children is a means of controlling them, or continuing their dependence on you by making you indispensable to them.

When the boundaries of independence and dependence become confused, and when parents begin doing too much for their children to the point of feeling overwhelmed, they often stop taking good care of themselves. Not taking good care of themselves, they become more susceptible to the effects of being overtired or overtaxed, which in turn leads to the possibility of anger, fear, self-pity, depression, and chronic tiredness. Parents in these states cannot exercise good judgment about their children's needs; nor can they provide healthy examples of respect for personal needs.

Ultimately, the example of our own behavior is the most dynamic gift we give our children. If we want our children to learn to be independent, we must learn to be independent ourselves by developing personal responsibility to ourselves. In a recent conversation with my daughter, I learned that she was influenced more by the way she heard my friend and me talk about dieting and exercising than by all the good things I had told her about her body. She had thought that our bodies were perfect; but with all our fussing, she learned to fuss and worry over her perfect body too.

We have probably all seen the mama cat who weans her kittens gradually. First, she is ever present. Later, she nurses them regularly, but jumps up in the middle of feedings to go off and do something else. Finally, she goes so far as to swat her kittens away from time to time. While I don't advocate the swatting, I do realize that the mama cat understands the give and take of love. Humans, on the other hand, sometimes go to the extreme of either pushing love away ("I'll do it myself") or pulling it in ("I'll do it for you").

As parents, we don't want to insist that our children become prematurely independent, and so we don't teach them to push away from those they need in order to please them. But neither do we want to be so dependent on pleasing them that we create codependency. It is the daily activities of ordinary life with our families that provide the stuff of personal transformation. A real transformation occurs when we are willing to meet the needs of the dependent child while still acknowledging our own needs, and when we are able to entrust the child to the world while still providing a safety net. This is the push and pull of love.

Birth: A Powerful Focus

Having a baby is a powerful experience that elicits strong emotional responses from all involved. Childbirth advocates bemoan the medicalization of childbirth, the high cesarean rate, and the malpractice crisis. Parents grieve over unexpected birth experiences. Some mothers see themselves as victimized by those who they expected would take care of them; others do everything "right," read the practical and inspiring literature, and attend births. For all these women, the outcome of birth is not predictable. Birth is normal, but it is never the same. And it is not simple to identify one way to prepare all women for normal childbirth.

Childbirth preparation must come of age. We have strong models for the way we want to give birth, and we know full well the impact of the birthing experience on the new family. At our disposal, however, are mostly intellectual tools. And birth is not an intellectual experience; birth is a transformative event on many levels. If one welcomes this transformative element during pregnancy, and responds to the growth and change that it brings, perhaps birth itself can necessitate less of a personal upheaval.

Birth is unpredictable by nature. The best way to prepare for it is to become skilled at handling the unexpected. The very best preparation for women approaching childbirth may be some type of rite of passage in the form of a wilderness or survival experience—a surrender experience. In a surrender experience, one learns to rely on inner resources, to trust the body's responses, and to develop quick and decisive thinking under

stress. Although a woman may know intuitively that birth is
normal, she must still find a way during pregnancy to awaken
the body to full confidence in its ability to meet the challenge of
labor and to birth normally.

Trusting one's body also means relying on the body, believing in the body, and knowing what to do when limitations
arise. Women often ignore vital bodily messages; they may
delay the body's need to urinate or defecate, avoid menstrual
blood, or feel uncomfortable about nakedness. These habits are
windows into the mind's degree of respect for the body. As
such, they provide opportunities for learning about one's body
in an effort to fully accept the powerful physical focus of childbirth.

A woman develops trust in her body by getting to know it in
operation. Engaging in a vigorous physical project at the beginning of pregnancy—digging a well, chopping weeds, garden-
ing, or building—can help focus the psyche on bodily strength,
the ability to accomplish new tasks, and the capacity to stretch
physical boundaries. This initial project can be augmented
throughout pregnancy by such ongoing physical activity as
movement, dance, yoga, walking, or swimming. Through eager
involvement in physical activity during pregnancy, a woman
develops a relationship with her body that can help her recognize important cues during labor.

As a culture that discounts the body, we often lack a vocabu-
lary that helps us access parts of the body. Knowing this vocab-
ulary, we can feel comfortable in our body and comfortable
with the language used by birth practitioners. Anatomy and
physiology textbooks and touching experiences such as massage, acupressure, and Rolfing can sharpen one's ability to
focus on the body.

A woman's birth experience mirrors her life. Labor, as a peak
experience, can be an intense microcosm of her unfinished business. Although it would be unrealistic to expect to transform all
aspects of life in preparation for birth, simply identifying per-

sonal attitudes and beliefs can help enormously. If, for example, a woman is routinely intimidated by authority figures, she can change this reaction during pregnancy; she can choose a birth attendant who is not intimidating or find a labor coach who understands her reaction and is prepared to supply a different response. If a woman tends to blame others when problems occur and to feel victimized when things go wrong, she can examine issues of control and work on developing high self-esteem and feelings of powerfulness during pregnancy. Anticipating areas of strength and making plans to get help in areas of weakness will keep the birth focus strong. If birth is a metaphor for life, the dynamics that are true for your life will be true for your birth.

Our beliefs and attitudes about birth are learned mostly from childhood stories and experiences. Children of birth practitioners, for example, often get mixed messages about birth. Birth is wonderful on the one hand; but the dramatic births often get talked about the most, and birth takes Mommy or Daddy away unexpectedly. The way we think about birth and the way we expect it to be are further shaped by our own birth recollections, our view of women in general and of the women in our family in particular, and our feelings about sex, pregnancy, pain, authority figures, doctors, midwives, hospitals, fear, and the display of emotion. Examine these beliefs with a friend or partner, and give special attention to how you deal with fear of the unknown, what you fear the most, and how comfortable you are expressing strong emotions among people you do not know well.

The practice of meditation and the practice of mindfulness that develops through meditation speak to the spiritual, transcendent nature of birth. Meditation, as well as the breathing techniques taught by contemporary childbirth methods, enhances the ability to focus at will, and this ability can be used to stay in the moment during contractions. As meditation and breathing are practice for the intense focus of birth, so is the act of making something for the child practice for devotion to the real baby. This act of devotion focuses the mother's thoughts on the baby and, by making the baby more of a reality, instills a sense of readiness for the birth.

Women who welcome ceremonies of celebration during pregnancy, such as showers or blessingways, invite support from the larger community. The mother and father may want to keep a journal during pregnancy, a record of dreams or of personal or shared thoughts. Balance this serious, thoughtful preparation with playing and singing. Playing keeps the soul hopeful and lessens reliance on the intellect. And singing relaxes the singer. Singing and laughing involve the whole body, as does childbirth; and relaxing the muscles of the face and jaw relaxes the muscles of the vagina. Sing. Sing. Sing.

If, during pregnancy, we regularly examine our beliefs and attitudes about life, we are sure to confront our beliefs about fear and pain. Do we believe that if we do it right, childbirth "should" not be painful? Do we believe that if we are in top physical shape, labor will be shorter? Do we think that a wonderful diet will spare us unnecessary inconvenience? If we feel prideful about our childbirth preparation, we may feel let down when childbirth does not proceed as anticipated.

Whether or not childbirth should hurt does not matter; the point is to know how to approach it if it does. What inner resources will we rely on? How willing will we be to trust our body? How determined are we to accept the fullness of the birth experience? Birth is likely to be more than we anticipate, but it need not be more than we can handle.

The intellectual framework of childbirth education provides necessary information on the history of childbirth and childbirth reform, of breathing methods in childbirth, birth options and practitioners, and consumer choice. But we need more. We need bodies that are trained to respond to minds, comfortable and knowledgeable about themselves, and are willing to surrender to birth. We need honest self-appraisal that acknowledges personal strengths and strives to accommodate for personal weaknesses. And we need women engaging in full body awareness, willing to see birth as a metaphor, and preparing to process it as it happens, with deep inner trust in the larger meaning of life. It is the powerful focus of these women that will transform birth as we know it, by refusing unnecessary cesareans and interventions and by refusing to see themselves as victims of birth.

The Gift of Conflict

In recent times, the American people have witnessed intense scrutiny of public figures by an overzealous media. The careers of political figures and television evangelists have ended because their sexual behavior did not correspond with the public's view of morality. Our society is willing to chastise and reject people for their sexual imperfection while overlooking the moral imperfection of world leaders who sanction subterfuge and violence in the name of democracy.

As a culture, we are confused about our personal sexuality while obsessed with sex and violence in advertising, television, and films. The hostility and rejection showered on public figures who err sexually is evidence of the emotional distress that has its roots in our rejection of the physical in particular, and of imperfection in general. We are willing to condemn others because we are ultimately willing to condemn ourselves.

The impossible standards that we have created for public figures underscores a belief that perfection in action is possible, that perfection is something to be earned rather than something we are born with. Our innate perfection and preciousness need not be proven. As humans, we will sometimes err, however, and our errors in judgment will sometimes result in conflict with others.

A common response to conflict, as evidenced by these media witch-hunts, is to avoid it altogether by rejecting the offender. This serves to protect our own beliefs by avoiding confrontation with challenging beliefs. At the same time, this willingness to reject assumes that the other is inferior and that it is possible to live without mistakes. It supports the belief that perfection is something to be achieved, rather than the nature of who we already are.

In family life, this can translate into an avoidance of conflict with our children or our mates, because conflict would imply that someone is wrong and someone is right. We know from our own experience as children that being "wrong" can result in pain. If we were punished or hurt for doing things we did not know how to do better and therefore *could not* have done better, we learned to avoid conflict at all costs. Rejection of conflict has at its root the belief that there is one right way of doing things.

When we are frightened of conflict in the belief that it implies blame or failure, we will try to avoid or deny it. One way to avoid conflict is to take responsibility for it and try to fix it. If conflict is unnecessary, if someone is always to blame, and if that someone might be me, then fixing it quick is one way to get rid of it. If there's a mess in the kitchen after the children have made cookies, it just might be Mom or Dad who are at fault for not disciplining the children better . . . or it might just be the way children are.

Another way to avoid conflict is to give ourselves up in martyrdom. "Poor me, I have to clean up the children's mess again!" The parent who feels victimized when the children have simply behaved like children often believes that with better parenting, the children might have behaved better.

We can also choose to act undisturbed in the face of conflict, to act uninvolved and indifferent as though it really doesn't matter if the kitchen drawers stick together or the kitchen floor is slippery with flour. To live in situations that are intolerable to our personal sensibilities because we cannot tolerate bringing up our own needs is the extreme avoidance of conflict.

Taking inappropriate responsibility for situations, feeling sorry for ourselves, and acting indifferent are all ways to avoid conflict—conflict that may be necessary to teach our children new skills that will neither deny their real abilities nor try to turn them into little adults.

Our willingness to reject others who are different, or political figures who make errors in personal judgment, stems from our willingness to condemn ourselves and to hide our own imperfections. If life is for learning, then conflict is inevitable. What conflict really implies is that we've met an obstacle, a boulder in the middle of the road, that reminds us to readjust our biocomputer and set a new course. When we see conflict this way, and see that throughout life we learn from conflict, we can remain open to it. When we do not fear conflict, and trust in the appropriateness of *all* events in our lives, we can remain available and caring to those we come into conflict with, and we can choose a loving way to resolve the problems.

When we believe that conflict is just the way it is, rather than assuming someone is at fault, we can offer help and information without any strings attached. We can tell the cookie makers that they might get a shock by sticking the knife in the toaster, and remind them that the honey is ruined for other uses when it has butter in it, and even offer to help them clean up the mess without imagining that our assistance will undermine their budding sense of responsibility.

Having relinquished the controlling behaviors used to avoid any possible pain that conflict may cause us, we can ask our loved ones what part our behavior plays in a problem, and then make adjustments. You may find, for example, that your husband doesn't take more responsibility for household maintenance because you jump in and "fix it" before he has a chance to act, or that you have such high standards for his performance that he has no room for learning and growing.

Perhaps the most helpful way to respond in conflict is to tell others how their behavior is affecting us. I have found that projecting self-pity and self-righteousness for being the family servant has much less impact than telling my husband how overwhelmed I feel planning Christmas presents and holiday celebrations by myself. It is essential to share such reactions without making others feel guilty or responsible for our feelings, and this comes more easily when we understand that conflict is not anyone's fault.

To share these feelings, we have to let go of pridefulness, that part of ourselves that doesn't want to admit that we, too, might have something more to learn from life. And to build the self-esteem needed to let go of pride, we must be willing to admit to our mistakes and imperfections, while still recognizing that we are doing the best we can at any time. The love between oneself and one's family must be assumed. If our loved ones believe that our love for them is dependent on what they do rather than on who they are, they will live in constant fear of a conflict that will finally prove their unworthiness.

We are all worthy of love, if only because we breathe life. We need not prove our essential worthiness or perfection to one another by our actions. Our political figures can be judged not by mistakes that reveal their personal pain, but by qualities that indicate their suitability for leadership. Other countries can be judged not by their form of government, but by the common bond of humanity that we share with them as members of the world family. And our loved ones can simply not be judged.

When our families challenge our patience, as they will and must, we can refuse to see conflict as a reflection of our own inadequacy, and thus something we must protect ourselves from. Instead, we can focus on our love for them and our own innate goodness. We can trust that conflict will once again, as it always does, give us a fresh perspective. We can choose to offer help, give information, resolve our part in the problem, and share our feelings without holding onto hidden agendas. The hope for conflict resolution lies in our willingness to hope and to admit to who we are. When we choose what is truly loving to ourselves, it will always be loving to others.

An Ethic of Parenting

The attention given to the accoutrements of birth—the baby clothes and baby carriers, the room where baby will sleep, even the place of birth and birth attendants—often distract us from the vital need for developing, above all, an ethic of parenting.

An ethic of parenting can help us to be creative rather than reactive in our parenting, and can prepare us to answer the moral questions that arise once a real baby enters our life. These are moral questions because the way we answer them will determine the way in which we interact with our child, and the way we interact with our child will have lifelong effects. Our ethic of parenting will determine, for example, whether we see ourselves in an adversarial or a cooperative relationship with our child, and this perception will underlie the relationship from birth to adulthood.

An ethic of parenting must be based on who the child is, on the true nature of the child, and on what we really know about the human child. It must not be based solely on the prevailing beliefs of the culture, because such beliefs are too arbitrary, transitory, and tenuous to sustain an ethic that will determine, to a large extent, the life history of an individual.

One of the cultural beliefs currently in transition concerns the place of women in the home and in society. In traditional tribal societies, the roles of women were integral to the functioning of the community. The life of the community depended upon the partnership of men and women. Today, though, we speak of equal rights for women—a concept that can only exist when

73

such partnership has lost its meaning. Being a mother is not valued in our society. The economic contribution of a woman at home is not valued in our society. A woman whose worth is defined by society appears to have little choice but to look to money and success as markers of her value.

I believe, however, that women will never be satisfied with an economic imitation of men's lives. Women must find a new way, a way of the spirit, and they must insist on an economic reality that acknowledges the concerns of the heart. If women are content with finding success as men have found it—in the marketplace away from home—we will never create a better world. When women polarize over daycare and at-home mommies, they polarize over a male model of the separation of work and family that has not worked for men and is not now working for women. It doesn't work—not because we need more daycare centers, but because the current social reality we emulate has no heart.

We must seek broader solutions to the economics of family life, and we must be very careful not to fall into the trap of defining ourselves solely by the values of a society in transition. An ethic of parenting based on the values of a society gone mad with materialism will have no substance, will be difficult to justify, and even more difficult to sustain. If we evaluate the success of an individual only by what he or she produces, then we will embrace daycare, early learning, and designer clothes for children. But we know that the obsession for materialism has produced inequality in the richest nation in the world; more than enough bombs to destroy the world; and a population deep in despair. We must be careful in adopting an ethic of parenting not to adopt without question the values of a society that we ourselves question.

If the culture does not define the child, then how do we do so? We look at the child, and we look at others who have looked at the child. We take a broad view, and we examine all the data. And then we come to our own conclusions. Always, we must perform a leap of faith, a synthesis in consciousness, before making the philosophy our own; otherwise, we will be subject to the opinions of ever more convincing authorities. Once our ethic of parenting has been integrated within us and assimilated in a personal way, we will be able to extrapolate it into all new situations.

When we look at the broader data, far beyond the studies of daycare conducted over the last decade, we see a number of common threads. We see that emotionally stable, cooperative, tribal societies have all supported close, intimate, sensual contact and prolonged breastfeeding between mother and child. We see that animal mothering behavior falls into two categories: cache and carry. Species in the cache category are stashed in a den with other offspring while their mothers look for food, do not need to feed often because their mothers' breastmilk is high in fat content, and do not need frequent physical contact with the mother. Species in the carry category, on the other hand, are marsupiallike. Their mothers' breastmilk is low in fat content and must be consumed almost continuously. They are not born in litters, and close physical contact with the mother not only ensures frequent feeding, but also stimulates brain development. Humans are a carrying species.

John Bowlby studied the effects of extreme maternal deprivation in orphanages during the war years. Infants who were fed and kept clean, but not interacted with, did not live. He found that the basic human requirements of interaction and relationship were necessary for life to continue. Marshall Klaus and John Kennell, after studying the effects of early contact between mothers and infants, found that mothers who bonded well with their infants in the hours and days following birth were more securely attached to their infants months later. Selma Fraiberg linked the development of conscience to the love for the mother, as it is love for the mother that tempers the aggressive urge in human children. Rudolf Steiner and Joseph Chilton Pearce have both observed that the human infant learns by way of a matrix system. During the first seven years of life, the child is bonded to the matrix of the mother and attempts to alleviate discomfort by seeking this matrix.

People will say that we cannot measure the quality of life, so we cannot know which early experiences help to create an ego strong enough to endure unhappiness and healthy enough to enjoy happiness. I disagree. Evidence abounds in support of the basic human dyad of mother and child as fundamental to later human happiness. We all accept that an animal whose dyad is upset will not be fully animal, and we know that humans whose dyadic relationships are extremely upset never reach their potential. It is only a matter of extrapolation to suggest, at the very least, that we be highly cautious when we mess with the biological imperative of the mother-child dyad. In developing an ethic of parenting, have the courage to look at both human and animal families, and recognize the links of survival that have served life for centuries.

Once we have examined the broad data and drawn our own conclusions, we will come up against our personal limitations. The ethic of parenting that we develop may be very different from the way we were parented, very different from the way the majority of children in our society are parented, and very different from our inner messages about spoiling children and letting them run our lives. In our society, we are not accustomed to the surrender and service required by the human infant. To sustain an ethic of parenting that honors this surrender and service, we must surround ourselves with the kind of support and information that will help us overcome the limitations imposed by the way we ourselves were parented.

Ground your beliefs about the child in a larger reality, a personal myth, or a spiritual overview that does not alienate but rather joins you to others. Realize that beyond the personae of mother and child is the core of Personal Spirit, and that the journey on this earth is a journey of the soul. Serve your child—for in serving your child, in trusting your child, you serve yourself and give yourself an opportunity to be reparented and reloved. The greatest kept secret in the world is the personal transformation inherent in developing an ethic of parenting that is truly in keeping with the nature of the child. Parenting with this type of ethic releases the full potential of the human being, a force greater than anything we have yet seen on this planet.

For a Better World

S ister Joan Derry, BK, and other members of the international order of Brahma Kumaris have visited cities all over the world asking people for ideas for a better world. The project is cosponsored by the United Nations and will culminate in a presentation of these ideas before the UN. How refreshing to focus on solutions rather than problems, although in so doing, one realizes how much more difficult it is to solve problems than to complain about them.

Thinking about solutions requires that we believe a solution is *possible*, that we take responsibility for helping create that solution, and that we recognize how even the subtlest details of our daily lives are either part of the problem or part of the solution. How is my willingness to ignore a homeless person in a deserted doorway of my hometown related to the problem of poverty and homelessness in society? How is my inner peacefulness and the peace I do or do not exude to others related to world peace? How is the way I raise my children a reflection of the values I hold for the future of our planet?

I believe that if we raise our children well, all the rest will fall into place. Raising our children well, however, is a complex endeavor. It means that we as parents believe in and respect the integrity of each child's inner experience of life. It means that we do not try to impose an arbitrary outer authority on our children and thereby teach them to doubt their inner reality and depend upon outside approval for self-esteem. In a better world, a child's personal experiences of life will not be denied, trivialized, or ignored by adults in deference to some superior,

rational, intellectual, and controlled reality. Adults will delight
in the childishness of children—in their weakness, their vulner-
ability, and their innocence—and will protect them and cherish
them. As a result, children will grow up trustful of their own
experiences and proficient in balancing these inner experiences
with the experiences of others. They will be skilled problem
solvers.

In a better world, children will grow up with self-respect and
self-esteem, and will therefore create solutions for ecology,
defense, human rights, apartheid, poverty, birthing, and relationships that respect the personal experiences of others.
Knowing the inner balancing act that occurs among ideas, sen-
sations, intuition, and valuation, they will create solutions that
reflect a balance of these functions rather than a battle among
them for supremacy. Trusting inner valuation from an early age,
they will instinctively know the difference between inner value
and outer judgment.

In a better world, society will recognize that time spent raising children is worthy of an individual's best efforts and is worthy of society's full support. A better world will know without
a doubt that the future of any society is dependent on how it
values its children. The society that values children will provide
families with support that is more broadly based and more creative than the current dichotomy between "quality" daycare
and mothers at home; it will embrace a wide spectrum of occu-
pational and economic options, all of which acknowledge that
parents and children need to be together, need to prioritize this
relationship, and need to access support from others, especially
during the intense early years of parenting.

In a better world, children will be welcome in public. The
business community will realize that serving families is good
business. When traveling or shopping with children, it will be
easy to find airports, restaurants, and businesses where children are treated with respect, where bathrooms for children and
changing tables for babies are standard fare, where children's

play areas are available, and where older children can make a
phone call or receive assistance when lost or afraid.

In America, we often expect the government to solve our
social problems, and we look with envy at the extensive social
programs in Europe. Changes in America will come from the
private sector, however. Employers will develop creative work
options for their employees, welcome children in the workplace, and offer maternity and paternity benefits that will truly
help families. This is citizen diplomacy, and it begins at home.

In a better world, everyone in the community will be knowledgeable about birth and breastfeeding. We all will have
learned that birth is normal and pregnancy is not a disease, and
we will look back in amused wonder at the bad old days of
excessive medical intervention in the natural process of
birthing. Everyone will know that a woman's body can be trusted, that birth is safe, and that many birthing options exist; and
our healthcare system will acknowledge homebirth as the standard of care. Hospitals will provide emergency medical backup
for homebirths, and midwives working in both home and hospital settings will be the cornerstone of maternity care.

Every woman in the world will be assured of sensitive prenatal care, good healthy food during pregnancy and lactation, a
supportive birthing environment, and help at home during the
postpartum period. Infant mortality statistics will be a thing of
the past, as all countries will have solved the problem of unnecessary infant deaths through a cooperative international effort
spearheaded by such organizations as the United Nations, the
World Health Organization, the International Homebirth movement, the International Federation of Midwives, the Midwives
Alliance of North America, the American Foundation for
Maternal and Child Health, and *Mothering* Magazine.

In a better world, we will see ourselves as members of an
international community, as citizens of the world. We will come
together with people of like interests in other countries as easily
as we now come together with people of like interests in other

states. No longer defining ourselves by geography or economics, we will choose our friends, our music, our food, our occupations, and our pastimes from a rich and abundant international palette. And, in a better world, no people will be enemies.

What we are undergoing in the world today is a crisis in perception. Our institutions do not reflect the way we experience life. We believe the family should be one way, and yet our experiences reveal a wide variety of ways of being family in the world. We believe that as the richest nation in the world, we should have everything; but the homeless remind us of the inequality of wealth in this country, and the newspaper headlines tell us that money does not buy happiness. And we have believed for too long that someone else would take care of things if we were good enough. In a better world, we will all grow up, face the problems of the world without worrying about who created them, and solve them one by one.

In a better world, we will understand that our purpose here is greater than we know. We will realize that we are coevolving the species and that to do this we must make creative solutions based on inner experience rather than outdated ideation. In a better world, the children we have raised to trust their inner experience will create new institutions that truly reflect this inner reality. A better world will have enough of everything for everyone, because the children will have grown up believing that there is enough of everything for them.

Ever a Becoming

"**M**uchness" is the best word to describe the state of my life and the lives of those around me. Cars are breaking down; people are moving; canyons are flooding; relationships are ending and beginning; careers are changing; and almost everyone is talking about making more money, and moving too fast. Some vaguely attribute this sense of upheaval to the Harmonic Convergence, to a purification by fire that the earth may now be experiencing, or to the last stand of materialism. If nothing else, we become more aware of the process of life we are in when our goals seem obscured and beyond reach.

A friend who is going through several major life changes suggested that I write about change. Lately, change is all that I have been aware of. Life is changing. Always was. Life is always becoming. I have believed until recently that my life was moving toward a goal, toward an ever-increasing improvement based on my personal past performance, toward a reward for participating so well in the human race. In my mind, I saw life as a long, straight path toward a shining light.

While I still see the shining light, it moves now. I see that the light moves in and out, up and down, around and around. Sometimes it surrounds me; sometimes I cannot find it. So I have come to view life more as a changing process than as a movement toward a goal. The movement along the straight path is a coat that fits too tightly, that does not acknowledge the reality of change.

When I see life as a process, I want to learn from life rather than protect myself from it. When I see life as moving toward a goal, I protect myself from all aspects that deviate from my pre-scribed goal. Relationships, love, and conflict change dramati-cally when life is seen as a process. "An honorable human rela-tionship—that is, one in which two people have the right to use the word 'love'—is a process delicate, violent, often terrifying to both persons involved, a process of refining the truths they can tell each other," says Adrienne Rich. "It is important to do this because it breaks down human self-delusion and isolation. It is important to do this because in so doing we do justice to our own complexity. It is important to do this, because we can count on so few people to go that hard way with us."

When I believe that life is goal oriented, I berate myself if things go wrong, I take life personally, and I continually expect more of myself in an effort to fix things and make them better. When I believe that life is a process of becoming, I admit that life is sometimes beyond my control, that bad things happen to good people, and I ask myself questions about what is happen-ing to me as I would ask questions about any new subject I am learning about. In a conflict situation with a loved one, child or adult, I ask myself: "What good reason does _____ have for his or her behavior?" "What can I learn from this situation?" "What am *I* getting from this situation?" "What do I believe about this situation?" "What personal issues or areas of difficulty come into play in this situation?"

I used to believe that unconditional love meant acting loving toward others no matter what they did. This implied that I had to act lovingly despite their unacceptable behavior. I was un-able to acknowledge my angry feelings because anger implied lack of loving. If I was "supposed to" be loving them no matter what they did, and I got angry at their behavior, then I was either not loving them enough or not loving myself enough to learn how to anticipate my anger, count to 10, and avoid it.

Anger just is. Unconditional love does not mean liking every-thing a loved one does. That is impossible in any state of con-scious individuation. Rather, unconditional love is the ability to

handle ambivalent feelings about the loved one. Love is something we bear the suffering of. Love is a stormy feeling. When
we cannot handle the storminess, the suffering, or the ambivalence that love brings up, we try to control the situation and the
one we love. And when we are controlling, we are seeing life as
a product rather than a process.

Once we can handle our ambivalent feelings and relinquish
control, then we can find new choices for resolving conflict with
loved ones. We can offer help and information without any
strings attached. We can resolve the part we may have in the
problem. We can explain how the person's behavior is affecting
us, without trying to make the person feel guilty or responsible
for our feelings. We can address, rather than withdraw from,
the conflict.

Love is an action, and those who translate love into action
are best at loving. Children make no separation between feeling
and acting. Their spontaneity and candor challenge our consciousness. Children act according to what they value, and they
know what they value. They choose their play, food, and clothing based more often on what they value than on what they
"should" value. By loving them, we can learn to act in accordance with our own values, not only our ideas. If what we value
is relationship with those we love, then we will recognize and
make time for the process of the relationship at least as often as
we make time for the things we "have" to do.

We are continually redefining personal boundaries. We are
continually differentiating between the many stimulations and
temptations our culture has to offer. Amid such emphasis on
consumption and production, it is easy to lose one's way with
family and loved ones. I have been a parent for 14 years, and
still ask myself if I am spending as much time with my family
and my loved ones as I want to. Does the time I spend with
them really reflect the value I place on them? Am I remembering to *live* life in the midst of the demands of living?

Humor has become a necessity. I have had to develop a

repertoire of activities—art, music, making things, beauty, ritu-al, spiritual practices, dances, songs, special places, smells, sounds, stones, flowers, water—that can soothe the terror of letting go of situations I never had control of in the first place. Learning to live life as it happens and to value the process however it unfolds requires that I live life as a remembrance—that I remember who I am. I want to continually remember that we are beings moving unevenly in the light rather than beings competing for it.

As we engage one another in cooperative relationships that assume change, assume differences, we share responsibility for problem solving. We can also share our common suffering and agree that joy is our birthright, not only our just reward.

Keeping Hope Alive

A friend calls to say that her baby in utero has an extremely serious heart defect. She must choose between the almost certain death of the baby in a homebirth that the heart could not survive and the almost certain death of the baby after a series of emergency operations, some done without anesthesia. Another friend suffers in a seemingly happy marriage that no longer sustains her emotionally, because she fears the impact of divorce on her children, her husband, her friends, and herself. She must choose between herself and her marriage. A third friend keeps the fact that she is gay from her family and some of her friends. In coming out of the closet, she must choose between her personal integrity and the loss of her family and friends. Impossible choices. How does one make them? How does one find the strength to face what is, do what has to be done, and keep enough hope alive to make impossible decisions? How do my friends find where hope lives for them in each of these situations?

We are afraid of the blackness of life, of the times that feel like endless nights, of the sadness that is as much a part of life as is the joy. We can take back the night of our darkest moments with faith, hope, and charity. As a Catholic child, I knew these as the three theological virtues, and I wore a gold bracelet with a cross, an anchor, and a heart to remind me of these virtues.

We can take back the night with charity: with a love of God, of something greater and bigger than ourselves that can comfort us in the night; with a willingness to transcend the pain while still living through it; and with a love of ourselves that

86

mediates our need to be approved of by others. We can take back the night with faith: with an acceptance that the fullness of life includes the rapture of pain, the ecstasy of suffering, and the validation of *all* of life's experiences. And we can take back the night with hope: with an abiding hope that the darkness will reveal something of the magic and mystery of life that will enrich and inspire us, and with hope in the possibility of a brighter day.

I feel hopeful when I can see solutions. When I can't, I panic or move into depression. I go into high gear until the hope resurfaces in the form of one small step that makes a fine rift of light in the curtain of darkness. That step may be minuscule; but it is something I can do, and it gives me hope. To break the bondage of the darkness, I have come to learn how to activate hope.

When I need hope, I might call in humor to help me laugh and forget myself long enough to relax into the mode of the heart, in which everything is possible. When I need hope, I bring in helpers. The possibility that something is beyond my personal resources does not mean that it is impossible to handle, because I can collapse into the arms of my friends who buoy me up and take over for a time, or symbolically support me in my suffering. I can bring in prayer. I can ask for inner help from the Divine Comforter or from the gods and goddesses who inhabit me, or demand that the clamor of the unconscious be silenced awhile, or simply ask to do God's will. I can be recharged by the inner faith that everything happens as it should. Life happens as it should simply because it *is* what is happening.

I have feared that my son born with a cleft lip and palate would not hear; I have feared that my 5-month-old daughter with spinal meningitis would not live; I have feared that I would never make it through another night with a sleepless teething baby; I have feared that my 10-year-old son would never read; and I have feared that the daughter I homeschooled for eight years would not adjust to high school. Only my hope in the future moves me forward into this uncharted territory of the human spirit.

When my pregnant friend finds the place within her heart that holds the reply to the question "What is life?" she will have her answer. When my married friend awakens the soul in her that demands growth above all else, she will have her answer. When my gay friend finds the fearlessness to define her life by who she is rather than who others assume her to be, she too will have her answer. Each of these people is being asked to step front and center in the nakedness of her raw self and face what life has to offer . . . recklessly, in fear and trembling. Their knees may be shaking, their hearts racing, but by facing life as it comes, they will learn they can go to hell and return again. They may be scorched, but not burned, by the fire.

By embracing the gray matter of life—the part that lives in the brain tissue, in the inner cavity of the body, in the seams between the black-and-white thinking of paternalism—I have found a way to live in life without controlling it. To live life without controlling it, I replace my bodily armor with precise, clear, and truthful personal boundaries. I have developed tools to survive the heat and return. I may be in uncharted territory, but I am held securely in the safety net of faith, hope, and charity.

The anchor of hope weighted by the faith in a greater good is forged by the charity of truthfulness. To endure suffering, we must be prepared to tell ourselves the truth about our own experiences. Even if we choose not to act on this truth, we must know what it is. We must be prepared to speak the truth in service to ourselves and those we love, because love is an action. We must choose our vision sources carefully. Whom do we trust? What do we believe? How do we protect ourselves from psychic pollution? Truth sets us free if we are courageous enough to look it in the face.

Another friend taught me that we can tell we are getting

close to our intent in life—that is, our own personal truth at the core of our being—whenever we experience fear, control, or denial. Fear has power we can use to our advantage by neither denying the fear nor being controlled by it. Feel the fear and act *with* it. Know that any time you are gripped by fear, overwhelmed by an intense desire to control a difficult situation, or denying that anything is even happening, you are on the verge of discovering and perhaps acknowledging some truth vital to your personal mission. Despite the fear, despite the suffering, there is hope. When you are speaking and living the truth of who you are, you are smack-dab in the middle of the ecstasy of life—right where you belong.

Schooling at Home

Fifteen years ago, when my first child was a baby, I began looking around at the educational options available in my community. I wondered about moving. I was interested in starting an alternative school, but there was not enough interest in our area to sustain it. About this time the first issue of John Holt's *Growing Without Schooling* newsletter arrived in the mail. My reaction to reading it was to heave a great sigh of relief. It confirmed my growing suspicion that learning didn't have to be difficult.

During those early years of examining educational options, I was not so much opposed to the public schools as I was simply *in favor* of learning at home. Learning at home was a natural evolution of our lifestyle. We were a family that was very much home oriented—homebirth, home business. Also in those early years, I learned that I could trust my children. Their perceptions of their experiences were accurate, and their experiences did not seem to indicate a desire for formalized learning. As I had been able to trust them to wean themselves and learn to crawl, walk, speak, and use the toilet, it seemed that I could rightly look to them for clues about when they were ready to learn to read and write. Then, too, I was not sure what the effect would be of formalized learning on their individuality at this young age.

I was concerned about separation from my children when they were young. Five or six years old seemed too early an age for them to leave home for long periods of time. It seemed that if my children spent 30 hours a week away from home, soon the values of their peers would supplant the values of our home. Certainly this supplanting is necessary at some point, but I believed that if it happened too soon, my children would be at risk.

I have four children: 15, 13, 11, and 7. All of them have been homeschooled. With each one, I have worried if he or she was getting a good enough education. In the early years of our homeschooling, we registered with the state as a private school and filled out simple paperwork twice a year. We gave our school a name and assigned formal grade levels because this made it easier for the children to answer people's questions about where they went to school and what grade they were in. We even had stationery, a logo, and a motto: "Every experience carries its lesson." We originally intended to use our private school as an umbrella for other homeschooling families, but during most years, we have had only four students at Sandhill Day School.

Over the years, I've gathered a lot of supplies. I particularly like to order from textbook companies because they have good photographs and descriptions of the books, and because you can order only a few books, teacher's editions, and workbooks. I've also gotten books and supplies from large office and school supply stores, and from public school book depositories. Sometimes schools give away old books. Universities often have resource libraries for teachers, where individual books and teaching aids can be checked out. Sometimes college level correspondence courses are appropriate for homeschoolers. Some of the better children's magazines have issues and supplements that can be used for lessons. I spend a lot of money on *good* quality art supplies for the children and take them to classes in drama, dance, singing, and art. These classes, plus our busy personal life, keep them in touch with friends; and because they homeschool with their siblings, they do not experience a sense of isolation. Homeschooling four children at once can challenge the individualized learning characteristic of the home environment, but the age spread in our family served us well: the two older children went on to school at a time when the younger two needed more attention academically.

Having been a teacher myself, I am sympathetic to the schools and to teachers, although I am critical of some modern educational practices. I believe that our society does not allocate enough money to education or appreciate how important the student-teacher ratio is. Nor do we fully appreciate that children learn from a living model. Homeschooling, as another option, underscores the diversity present in our population and the variety of educational choices that are possible. When we open ourselves to the dissidents in our society, when we appreciate and understand the homeschooling choice, we help to revitalize education in America.

Homeschooling represents a great leap of faith. Over the years, I have had to continually trust my children to learn what they needed, at their own pace. I had to trust that their early time of imaginative play and creative learning would give them a strong foundation for later, more abstract, study rather than put them at a disadvantage. And although I felt strongly that the socialization methods characteristic of the early years in school are often more harmful to children than helpful, I sometimes wondered if my children were meeting "enough" friends. It surprised me that what I thought of as a marvelous educational experiment was sometimes a source of embarrassment to the children.

Children do not know that society has the diversity that it does, and often adults don't seem to either. I have noticed, however, that my youngest child is particularly confident when asked about school. "Oh, I go to homeschool," she replies. No one flinches anymore. She certainly doesn't. During the 10 years that we have been homeschooling, we have experienced a great change in its social acceptability. Luckily, we live in a community where alternatives are common, so that while people may sometimes be surprised to hear about homeschooling, none are critical. In fact, most children who hear of it for the first time get excited and go home to ask their parents some challenging questions.

I have often wondered whether or not my children were at grade level in certain subjects. They have not learned to read or do square roots or play instruments at amazing ages. And while their accomplishments and their spirits astound me at times, I now see homeschooling as a contributor to that, not its cause. It has been important to temper my enthusiasm for homeschooling with my awareness of a need for balance. I have not wanted my children to feel inferior to their peers, or to be unnecessarily discouraged because they could not yet differentiate between their lack of rote skills and the lack of ability.

This became clear when my older two children entered school. My eldest daughter entered high school three years ago, after eight years of homeschooling. She had learned easily at home and had been presented with a diversity of material. She passed a test to enter a private school and was advised to take summer school math to prepare for the first year. Her first few months were a time of intense adjustment. Some days, I wanted to do her homework for her. She was adjusting not only to the new and challenging subject matter, but also to the realities of test taking, of sometimes puzzling school procedures, and of a newly school-centered social life. In time, school became manageable. By the end of the year, she had received high honors and done particularly well in math.

My eldest son entered a public junior high school after spending the last few months of seventh grade at an alternative school. He, even more than his sister, was eager for the social life that school seemed to represent. He had more catching up to do in major subjects, but he too managed to catch up quickly. The adjustment to the frenetic social scene has been as difficult as the adjustment to the academics. But then, for both children, the first day of school came a lot later than for most.

I don't think that homeschooling is a cause or a salvation. It has been a rich source of bonding and togetherness for our family, and I hope that for my children it will prove to be a strong foundation for later learning. The rising interest in homeschooling today shows that we as a society need to do a better job of educating the whole person. We also need to realize that whether one chooses homeschooling or formalized schooling, the parent needs to be involved in the child's learning. Just as I worried if my children were getting enough from homeschooling, so are other parents concerned about learning, regardless of setting, and seek the best education for their children.

Our increasingly complex society demands equally sophisticated technological skills and, consequently, solid human values. In the society of the future, we will need the ability to adapt to the unknown, the capacity to maintain personal balance in the midst of complexity, and the readiness to learn new things. Homeschooling both preserves the sense of learning as a vital and exciting experience, and places that learning in the context of personal and family life. It provides a model of learning for the future that will, more than most others, accurately reflect the diversity of who we are as a people as well as who we are as individuals. Hopefully, the question of the future will not be "What school do you go to?" but rather "What did you learn today?"

Homeschooling reminds us that learning is a fluid process. It is not fixed. It is a living process that cannot and will not be contained in a room or a book. We learn from the living model of life as it happens. The success of homeschooling reminds us that learning is simultaneously more fragile than we once thought and much easier than we often believe.

Who's in Charge?

I once believed that if I did everything "right" with my children—breastfed, homebirthed, actively listened, and didn't spank—I would be spared the turmoil associated with the teen years. I saw the teen years as some sort of war zone that I could avoid through virtue. But just as both joy and suffering happen to us all regardless of our virtue, so does the turmoil of the teen years happen to all families. Respecting your child as an individual will help, but it will not guarantee a smooth ride.

Several years ago, I went into a local ice cream parlor where punky-looking teens hung out. Just as I started to make a judgment on their clothes, their music, and their demeanor, I stopped short. *I* used to look like this, I realized. As a "heavy hippie," my attire had probably stood out even more than theirs, and yet I was harmless. Confused, seeking an identity, caught between two worlds, but harmless. Right then and there, I decided to learn to love rock and roll again. I vowed not to have those "Turn down that radio!" fights that are so common between parents and teens. Today, my children and I fight over what channel to listen to, and we flip back and forth among our favorite songs, but we all like rock and roll.

My return to rock and roll was a reasonable concession to harmless and necessary rebellion. Clothes, music, and hairstyle are personal choices that teens make to define themselves, and these preferences are harmless. My concessions to this harmless rebellion are appropriate. Other concessions are not.

Each of my children is unique and has been since birth. I have given them many choices in their lives, and we often make decisions democratically on matters that affect us all. But democracy has its limitations. Teens, new at making decisions, are faced with choices that have far-reaching ramifications, yet the healthy narcissism of teens often prevents them from taking into account the full spectrum of their needs and the needs of others. Often, it is only the parent who can see the whole picture.

Along with this healthy narcissism comes a healthy rebelliousness. "Why, Mom, why?" becomes the anthem of the early teen years—an echo reminiscent of the "terrible" twos. Although I have participated in the coming of teenage with two children, my experience with my son has raised some new questions. What is it like for a boy when he begins to grow taller and stronger than his mother? What kind of experience is it for this surging mass of hormones, this master of the universe, to be impeded by someone whose authority is no longer augmented by size and strength? For me, as a mother, it felt threatening, and I could no longer offer facile rationalizations for my decisions to this man-child who could outsmart and outrationalize me. I believe that my young buck's first challenge was to his mother.

I used to wonder why a student whom I knew in college was so demeaning and condescending to his mother. Now, I believe that the way a man treats his mother is an indication of the way he treats women in general. Does the boy-child whose mother gives up her authority as soon as he is taller and stronger learn to hate women? Does the boy-child who is not expected to do chores around the house because his other commitments are more important grow up to care for the baby and share household chores? In order to raise the next generation of birthing men, we must raise boys who do not feel superior to women, who know that strength is not equated with might, and who do not regard taking care of themselves as women's work.

I hear parents say that their teens need privacy, want to be alone, and that mothers and fathers are afraid to trespass.

Parents can interpret the surly, silent behavior of their teens as a personal rejection and abdicate their parental authority in the face of this onslaught, or they can interpret this behavior as a cry for help. Curiously, those teens who seem so independent, only because they are so distant, are often the ones who get into trouble. The honors student with numerous extracurricular activities is the one who surprises us with a drug or alcohol problem. Most parents seeking help from local parent assistance centers are not from poor, minority families, but rather from white, professional families whose children are modeling their parents' overcommitted lifestyles.

Because the decisions that my teens are now making—regarding driving, sex, drugs, and their futures—could be life-and-death decisions, they need my counsel. They do not need me to control them, but neither do they need me to relinquish them to the world. I sneak in minilectures in the car, in the kitchen, and around the house. I am confident that I have wisdom to share; but most often, I simply share my experiences. And I am careful not to take responsibility for my teens' actions or behavior.

I believe that a child whose parents abdicate their authority when challenged feels abandoned. It is the abandoned child who is wounded and who must act out as a rebel, a conformist, or a victim. This acting out creates clear boundaries within which to become an adult. When we assume that the teen who is surly and crabby wants to go it alone and does not need help, we give him or her a false sense of security and the message that problem solving is a solitary endeavor—that the adult solves problems alone. Our job as parents is to move our children from dependence to independence, but this movement occurs in fits and bursts, not in linear fashion or according to a timetable. Character and maturity develop, but they are not guaranteed by age. Only experience in self-regulation teaches self-regulation.

My children respond well when I have confidence in my

authority. I no longer accept arguments on matters of helping one another, sharing chores around the house, or disrespectful and unkind behavior. And I insist that my teens communicate with me so that they do not take out their school experiences on those of us at home. Peace in my home is not negotiable.

The teen years are a bridge from childhood to adulthood—a passage, a transfer of power. The teen walks the bridge, makes mistakes, plunges, holds back. The parents are the bumper rails along the sides of the bridge. The parents are available to bounce off of, but they do not do the walking. I can insist that my children respect my authority and my personal limitations because I have no ambivalence about my love, respect, and devotion to them.

As children challenge your authority, test your ways, and question your lifestyle, keep in touch. Don't be intimidated into giving up the authority that your position in the family requires, because if you don't claim your authority, someone else in the family will. And even if you are not wise, or do not feel wise, remember that your authority is not based on being right. It is based on who you are. You are the parent. You are the one in charge. That's the way it's supposed to be.

Changing Our Minds about Spanking

Our prisons are full. Despite incarceration, crime continues to increase. Punishment doesn't work, yet we rely on it. Overcrowded prisons remind me somehow of routine repeat cesareans and garbage dumps. Until recently, one cesarean meant an automatic second cesarean, and this contributed to an ever-increasing cesarean rate. Embarrassing birth statistics and consumer outrage have influenced the American medical community to rethink vaginal births after cesareans (VBACs), which are routine in many European countries. Excessive cesarean rates are related to excessive malpractice suits and to the mistaken belief that birth is by nature risky. Birth is normal.

We have dumped our garbage all over the world. Some of it floats around on barges waiting to be dumped. We cut down rain forests for hamburgers and American woodlands for Japanese houses. Although we use up resources at an alarming rate, we still haven't figured out what to do with what we've already used. Disposable products, dumping rather than recycling, and the quick use of resources are all based on the mistaken belief that nature is inexhaustible and invincible. Nature is fragile.

We punish people when they act harmfully in our society, and we punish our children in our homes and schools. In America, we sometimes even spank or paddle our children, although in some parts of the world this is considered a crime. We believe that punishment works. We also believe that spanking doesn't really hurt that much, that a little swat is incidental, and that what was done to us must be good for our own children, yet we fail to examine our own histories as children.

Punishment of children implies that they are stupid and mean and want to purposely hurt those they love. In fact, it is love that is the great motivator of socialized behavior. Only the bonds of love and trust forged early in the mother-infant relationship ensure a healthy conscience. Punishment, on the other hand, ensures hatred and revenge. The use of punishment with children is based on the mistaken belief that punishment changes behavior and that human behavior has to be controlled. Human beings are innately good.

Those of us who believe that spanking is necessary, or that it is OK to hit when we lose control, can change our minds. It is really a decision, after all. And learning what to do without spanking can only begin after the decision not to spank has been made. We will have to learn new responses: ways of intervening sooner and of mediating effectively. But first, the decision.

Violence is a learned response to conflict and an outmoded form of conflict resolution. Only recently have we learned to value communication. Communication was not mentioned in books about marriage until the 1950s, and childcare books from the early years of this century refer to people with different childcare ideas as "the enemy." Only recently have we brought consciousness to our interactions with children and seen them as more than possessions, servants, or little adults. As parents, we have the opportunity to reflect on the way we were parented ourselves and to observe and change habitual responses that are violent.

Although anyone who has spanked a child will wince at the likening of spanking to violence, it really is the same thing. Spanking teaches that we resolve conflict through physical means and that the strong can hurt the weak if the strong get mad enough or if the weak are deserving enough. It follows that individuals who, under certain circumstances, advocate physical means to resolve conflict in the home will also, under certain circumstances, advocate physical means to end conflict among nations. Our acceptance of violence among family members is our tacit approval of war among nations. As long as we are personally willing to rely on violence, we do not have to do the hard work that peaceful conflict resolution requires. Giving up violence and spanking means that we have to learn to talk to the ones we love . . . and the ones we hate.

In Lee Blessing's play *A Walk in the Woods,* a Soviet and an American diplomat negotiate an arms agreement. As they work out the details and the terms, it becomes evident that the possibility of an arms agreement hinges on the possibility of friendship. If these two people can become friends, then perhaps their countries can too.

If there are countries in which violence is rare, then perhaps there is a better, more civilized, and legally sanctioned way to deal with conflict. Law, after all, is an outgrowth of public opinion, and public opinion is a great socializer. Let us change our minds about spanking. Let us become a public opinion outraged at "small" acts of violence with far-reaching effects. In civilized countries, women and children are not victimized.

What effect does spanking have on the child? My children still remember their spankings even though I haven't spanked them in 10 years. A teenage girl I know recently attempted suicide in response to violence in her home. What does the child who is spanked or beaten do with the rage? I know adults who are still working it out in therapy. Alice Miller has documented the magnitude of destructiveness it precipitates on the road to maturity and beyond.

Do the children who are hurt or victimized in their homes grow up to hurt us back? Can we decrease simultaneously the violence in our society and the numbers of people in our prisons by refusing to be violent with children, ourselves, and each other?

Let's change our minds about spanking. Let's decide not to and find a better way. My children may play with GI Joes, but they stand in horror when they see an adult hit a child. I believe that the child who has not been hurt in the name of love will not grow up to hurt others with bombs or violence in the name of righteousness.

What Can We Do with the Moon?

A s Tom Robbins says in *Still Life with Woodpecker*, the last quarter of the 20th century is "a severe period for lovers." I once believed that couples were not trying hard enough to stay married. I believed that marriage was a matter of intention, not attention, and that if a couple was committed enough, it would work out. Last forever. Till death do us part.

I no longer believe it's that simple. Marriage is wonderful when it lasts forever, and I envy the old couples in *When Harry Met Sally* who reminisce tearfully about the day they met 50 years before. I no longer believe, however, that a marriage is a failure if it doesn't last forever. It may be a tragedy, but it is not necessarily a failure. And when a marriage does last forever with love alive, it is a miracle.

Love is a fluid process, and marriage is inherently ambiguous. As such, they both require care and maintenance. When we assume that marriage will automatically take care of itself, we may neglect to tend to it. The marriages that last with love alive are made of individuals who are willing to attend to and appreciate the marriage bond, not rely on it.

For the first time in history, communication has become the most important trait of a healthy marriage. Women have access to birth control; families are not dependent on marriage for economic survival; the media glamorizes sex, greed, and violence; and social values transform at an amazing rate. Rather than being aghast that so many marriages are ending, we might look in awe at how many are surviving or beginning anew.

I can speak about this because I am in the process of trying to

understand the end of my own marriage of 15 years and of
grieving its loss. Separation was a cry for help. Divorce under-
lined what had already happened. Love dies. Just as falling in
love "happens," so does falling out of love. For years, I could
not even acknowledge the situation because of the strong personal and public association I have of myself as a happily married person. I am still sorting it all out. I have a lot of questions
and few easy answers.

Is love a feeling or an action? I have a different experience of
inner worth when love is expressed to me in a facial gesture as
opposed to an action. And specific praise feels more loving than
does blanket reassurance. Love is a series of judgment calls
opening to new stages of evolution. Attraction, longing, lust,
falling in love, being in love. Each stage requires a judgment
call, determining whether or not the relationship will continue
to grow. As a young woman, I did not know that one could
bring judgment to love; I believed that attraction implied marriage. The requirements I have for love are different now, as a
42-year-old woman with four children, than they were when I
was a young, single woman.

Does commitment to marriage preclude all other commitments? How is commitment to self balanced with commitment
to marriage, especially when children are involved? Is an oath
to love another "until death" superseded by a prior commitment to self, even if that self is not fully recognized until after
the marriage? Must marriage sometimes be sacrificed to the
self? Can ailing marriages be healed? Is there always a choice?

It seems that the second half of life requires us to address the
unfinished business of the past. As the children grow up and as
making a living becomes more predictable, the marriage may
need to mature into a form that will support life without children again.

Can becoming a parent interfere with a marriage? One friend
said that his first wife became a mother and never came back.
Some of us immerse ourselves in mothering and forget our-

selves as women. Others discover, through mothering, a variety of personal needs that were never recognized before giving birth. Taking time out for oneself is necessary to develop a relationship with one's self, and having a relationship with one's self is necessary in order to have an intimate relationship with another.

Balancing self, family, and livelihood is the challenge of modern society. Blaming society for our problems only blurs the larger picture. What we need is a new view of marriage. As long as we expect that a marriage vow will take care of itself, or that relationship with others is possible without relationship to self, we will not give marriage its due in the later part of the 20th century. Marriage is for the brave. Old friendships and old marriages are miracles that happen to people who are willing to take emotional risks.

My friend tells me that her marriage of nearly 20 years has its ups and downs. Some years it's wonderful, and some years it's not. She accepts this as the "wave" of her marriage. Other friends who are discovering relationship without codependency tell me that they are able to maintain personal autonomy while surrendering emotionally. When marriage is not an economic necessity, a way of legitimizing children, or a confirmation of self-worth, what is it?

I have the most worrisome questions about children and divorce. For some time, I believed that my children's happiness was more important than my own. Children can recover from divorce if their inner male-female bridge is not damaged by the hostility of the separation, if they are kept informed, and if they are not abandoned and do not perceive themselves to be. Children need free access to both parents. Is it necessary to keep marriage together for children? What is more devastating for children—divorce or denial?

For the first time in history, we are asking what love is and looking at marriage as a beginning rather than an end, an adventure rather than an accomplishment. Love that endures is a miracle. Keeping love alive is like growing grass in New Mexico. Sometimes you look out at the lawn and see the beautiful green grass. Sometimes you look out at the lawn and see only brown spots. No matter what you see when you look at the grass, you always have to keep watering it. You always have to keep watering it.

Courage, Mothers, Courage

I n a recent mention of *Mothering* in *USA Today*, Deirdre
Donahue used the headline "Mother Courage" to describe
Mothering's environmentally conscious approach to issues
such as single-use diapers. I am struck by how accurately the
word *courage* describes mothering in general. It takes courage to
be a mother today, to be a woman who values mothering and
thinks for herself. It takes heroism.

The Welfare Reform Bill, signed by President Reagan before
leaving office, requires parents who are receiving Aid to
Families with Dependent Children (AFDC) benefits to find
work, if work is available, once their children are three years
old. Since a three-year-old child cannot be left alone, and since
few workplaces welcome children, parents with children over
three essentially receive money to pay others to care for their
children but receive no money to care for their children themselves.

Likewise, current childcare legislation favors subsidization of
institutionalized daycare. If the federal government sincerely
wanted to help families with child care, legislation would support families through tax credits, reimbursements, or direct
payments rather than through daycare assistance.

As if it weren't bad enough that legislation in this country
effectively penalizes the at-home mother, family support ranks
exceedingly low in comparison with other nations. Seventy-five
industrialized countries enact more legislation for families and
provide more money to offset the costs of parenthood. No
woman in Western Europe, for example, need ask who will pay

for her prenatal care. Only South Africa and the United States do not extend financial support for prenatal care, maternity leave, paternity leave, child allowances, single-parent assistance, and other family-related needs.

Furthermore, in 1987 the poverty rate for American families was 13.5 percent; for female-headed households, it was 34.4 percent. The average family income for mother-only households was about $12,000, while the average family income for father-only households was $24,000. Forty percent of the country's children are now living below the poverty-standard line.

Our pay scales reflect a time when men were the primary breadwinners. It is ironic that while women earn less money than men do for the same work, they are expected to financially support their children after divorce; whereas men, who are likely to earn more money than their divorced wives, are considered virtuous if they financially support their children after divorce.

Where in society do we see respect for the life of the home, the life of the spirit? Is there no longer any serious provision for this? How is the life of the home provided for? Who maintains the hearth? A fast-paced, technological society requires the strong individual to have an inner life, simply to balance the outer life. Can we step forth into a busy culture without having a quiet home life to return to? Can we do more by sometimes doing less? How can we balance the life of the intellect and the mind with the life of the heart and the senses? Do we know how to *be* as well as we know how to *do?*

These questions have traditionally been feminine ones—inquiries into the realm of relatedness, of order, harmony, and culture. It is the "woman's way" to value these questions because the woman's way is process. Women get the job done; however, they value the process along the way as much as the end result. As such, they value the hearth—not because it pleases the children or because it pleases the husband, but because it is pleasing in itself. It nourishes.

As Joseph Campbell said, "Raising a family is a meditation." Being a parent does not require trappings to make it a noble profession. I read recently of a book about iconoclasts, people who attack established beliefs and institutions. Curiously, only one woman was included in the collection. I realized, however, that mothers today are iconoclasts if they want to be with their children and make time for family life. Fathers, too, are iconoclasts when they jump off the daddy track into a rich home life.

What makes parents iconoclasts is that by valuing time for family and self, they erode the prevailing cultural myths that suggest "more is better" and "money buys happiness." Moreover, mothers who try to keep family first are the nobility of today. They are the nobility because they take care of the invisible. All that is really important is invisible: love, God, air. And because mothers take care of the invisible, they should be able to do so without trying desperately to fit this caretaking in between everything else.

Does society really need to be convinced that mothering is important? It is, after all, a biological imperative that we would never fail to recognize and support in any other species. A woman's body is designed to grow a baby inside and to feed that baby outside. It makes sense that society support this process to the best of its ability, because this process represents millions of years of cutting-edge expertise. Among animals—the cow and the calf, the horse and the foal, the duck and the duckling—we expect the relationship between mother and child to be protected by those in a position to do so. In human society, we must also expect this protection.

We know from adult psychoanalytic work that severe attachment disturbances occurring before age three contribute to psychoses and that those occurring before age five contribute to neuroses. Overwhelming evidence suggests that the relationship between mother and child be protected, at the very least, for the first five years. No doubt, a civilized society realizes that the success of the mother-child bond impacts on all future social service systems—medical, educational, business, and correctional—and that support of this early relationship improves all other relationships in society.

We have a diverse society of people with many cultural and racial backgrounds. Some people want children, and some do not. Some families want one balance of work and family life, and other families want another. Families can make up their *own* minds.

What we need are legislation and social programs that attack poverty, provide choices, and support the family unit. Eastern Europe is demanding self-determination. Tracy Chapman sings about "a city underground." My teenagers are listening to the Beatles. Process is making a comeback. Ideas and ideology are old news. *How* we are doing is now as important as *what* we are doing.

We will not succeed in improving our society or ridding it of drugs, moral decay, greed, graft, and lack of gaiety, until we begin to seriously support the fundamental processes of life. This means providing broadly based public and private supports for women and children. Everything in our society will start to make sense again when the last hungry child in America is fed.

Are We Done with Self-Righteousness Yet?

I am impressed by Czechoslovakian President Vaclav Havel's words spoken before Congress: "Without a global revolution in the sphere of human consciousness, nothing will change for the better in the sphere of our being. . . ." While others around the world are giving their lives for freedom of expression, those of us who already have it must look long and hard at what we do with ours.

I am disappointed by the self-righteousness I notice in the environmental and natural foods movements. Along with increasing concern for these issues, some people are beginning to believe that any action or feeling is justified as long as the cause is right. This type of thinking brings me back to my classical Catholic education: Does the end justify the means? What about the common good? The golden mean? Does a good cause justify rudeness, meanness, hatred, or self-righteousness? Dangerous stuff.

I heard one friend laugh with glee recently as he imagined those who "do not care about the environment" finally learning a lesson when the ocean water rises as a result of global warming and laps over their feet. I saw in his enjoyment of superiority a dangerous trend, because by then, it will be too late for us all. It is already too late for us to bask in feeling superior to others. Self-righteousness is outmoded.

Everyone is beginning to realize that we may have only a limited amount of time in which to reverse the disastrous environmental abuses that have characterized the last 50 years. If this is true, we can only reverse the trends by banding together without judgment to teach and help one another.

Our ability to teach and help one another rests on a willingness to embrace people with different beliefs. It is fair to assume that those who don't do anything about the environment either don't care about it or don't know any better. But believing they are uncaring jerks is dangerous. You then dismiss them and, in the process, become distracted from much of the real work you can do to improve things.

What we need now, more than anything else, is renewed hope. Hope that we *can* do something about the environment. Hope that we *can* raise healthy children. Hope that the earth *can* become a better, more humane place, where human rights are appreciated and protected and where we realize that we are not only residents of the earth, but also integral *parts* of it.

I like to think of the earth as a living organism, and authors have written beautiful books elucidating this point. If the earth is a living organism, perhaps the oceans, seas, and rivers are her blood; the land, her body; the trees, her arms. *And perhaps our consciousness is her consciousness.* What comes first: pollution of consciousness or pollution of the earth? We and the earth are so interconnected that it seems highly irresponsible at this critical juncture to use our mental imagery visualizing doom or disaster, or feeling superior to others. To me, pollution of consciousness is as offensive as a plastic diaper in a pristine lake.

I am sick of people making jokes about California falling into the ocean. I do not find these jokes funny. Many people I dearly love live in California. What comes first: thought or form?

We faced this question at *Mothering* recently, while discussing an environmental feature we are planning. Some favored lengthy explanations about the awful state of the earth and how we caused it, thinking that guilt would stop us. Others wanted solutions only, believing that we all know the causes but don't know how to make a difference. When I track my feelings, I realize that I am immobilized by guilt and can act only when I feel hopeful. After one of our editorial meetings in which we shared simple solutions that we use in our own lives, I came home, made separate bags for my recyclable garbage, and reduced the throwaway garbage for my family of five.

These themes run through the natural foods movement as well. Although I stopped using white sugar 20 years ago, just this year I bought some to make my grandma's Christmas cookies. I can use her recipes now, and as I do, I am flooded with memories of the smells of her kitchen. I add a little sugar to other recipes as well, because it really does work better at times. And, God forbid, I put sugar in my iced tea at restaurants. Have you ever tried to stir honey into iced tea?

I was inspired to lighten up by Jane Hirschmann's book *Are You Hungry?* (1986). Hirschmann believes that excessive prohibitions on food can be at least as damaging as the foods themselves. I have found this to be true. When my older kids started sneaking candy into the house in paper bags that they hid under their beds, I decided I would rather encourage the openness to explore both good and bad food choices than inspire guilt and furtiveness. So I removed all restrictions from food. At first, things that had never been in our kitchen began to find their way there—Oreos, Kool-Aid, ("Oh no, not *Kool-Aid!*"), sugared cereals, and candy cigarettes. At times, I was sure this openness was a big mistake, and I wondered if my youngest would ever learn discretion about sweets. Now, some months later I am pleased to say that nine bags of cookies sit opened but pretty much untouched in my cupboard. Juices are again as appealing as pop, and we're all beginning to get reacquainted with our old favorites.

One of my friends, who has struggled with food and weight issues all her life, understands what I am doing and says that this approach has given her the first moments of sanity about food that she has known. Another friend, whose young child goes nuts over the sugar choices in our house, drops hints about the content of Coke and apologizes for my sugar use in public. I wonder if it's the sugar or the prohibition of sugar that makes kids crazy around it.

All this goes back to freedom of choice and trust in the individual. I find it amusing that others suspect my motives, because I was for years a card-carrying member of the Look How Good I Am Because Of What I Eat Club. I gave up vegetarianism many years ago because I was choking on my own self-righteousness. I figured that was worse for me than meat.

In the wonderful book *Healthy Pleasures*, authors Ornstein and Sobel state that depression is a surer indicator of heart attack than are high cholesterol levels, high blood pressure, and cigarette smoking combined. People who seek and find pleasure in life live longer. Feverishly counting cholesterol, calories, and carbohydrates does not make for good health.

There is danger in fanaticism, even in fanaticism about good things. Self-righteousness leads to fanaticism, leads to fascism, leads to tyranny. The hatred engendered by right causes feels no different than racial hatred. We must say no not only to fascism as it has been played out in the countries of Eastern Europe, but also to the psychological underpinnings of fascism that lie in our willingness to feel superior to others. We must cleanse our psychic pollution as we clean up the earth. Then we can build a world in which it *is* self-evident that all people are created equal.

The Ecology of Raising Children

Step right up! Step right up! Get your designer baby strollers. Get your pinstripe baby carriers. Get your sequined baby tennies.

Fortunately, we have new products to entertain us, but when it comes to baby—less is more. And less is often all that is needed. New and better products do not necessarily make for better parenting any more than new and greener products will in and of themselves cure the environmental crisis. Short-term conservation and recycling goals are essential, but at the same time we have to implement long-term solutions. The best ensurance of long-term environmental protection is to grow up children who will *automatically* take care of the environment because they have been nurtured in ways that have taught them how to care.

We can encourage in our children those characteristics that we associate with environmental responsibility. We do not teach these traits directly, however. We teach them through our living model, and through the way we treat our children and ourselves.

Environmental consciousness refers to the inner as well as the outer environment. How we treat the earth relates to how we treat our bodies. How much we pollute our outer environment relates to how much we pollute our inner environment. How we treat our children relates to how we treat ourselves.

Environmentally conscious people can handle delayed gratification. They understand that a tree's history may be more important than its utility. Environmentally conscious people can put off short-term gratification for long-term satisfaction. Environmentally conscious people, however, are not martyrs. They understand that moderation endures and that repression breeds obsession. Environmentally conscious people are attached to their society and family. They have empathy for others, and they trust them. They do not feel isolated from society, and because they feel a *part* of something bigger than themselves they treat people and things as precious and protect them accordingly.

The qualities of attachment, empathy, and trust all develop during the first three to five years of life. It is not simplistic to say that a child who is treated as precious will treat the earth as precious and understand that his or her proper relationship to the earth is one of protection, not dominance. At the same time, a child who is treated as precious is not made to feel that he or she is the center of the universe.

Simple parenting choices have profound environmental overtones. Homebirth, for example, is the perfect ecological choice. It uses less technology, less energy, and less money than a hospital birth. Midwifery care, which underlies homebirth, is relationship rich and multidimensional. It provides a support net that protects against future technological interventions for both mother and baby and thus poses less environmental impact than other forms of care. Are we prepared to value that which is simple and costs less?

Breastfeeding is clearly an ecological choice. What could be more energy efficient than one person eating for two? Human milk is ideally suited for the human infant. No inorganic waste. No by-products, *no negative environmental impact*. We know that some women, either through personal choice or special circumstances, do not breastfeed. And we do not judge these women when we say that a mandate in support of breastfeeding deserves as much public support as the mandate in support of smoke-free public places. Breastfeeding provides overwhelmingly positive health benefits that continue long after the direct experience of breastfeeding is over. All institutions in our society should support breastfeeding as the ideal way to feed a baby and should extend that support beyond rhetoric and into real dollars.

The government currently buys about one-third of all infant formula manufactured in this country and gives it away to poor women. The WIC program distributes $449 million per year of free formula to poor women in this country. And formula companies make millions of dollars weekly selling artificial milk to women in Third World countries.

I would like to see the government put more money into breastfeeding than into formula-feeding. Successful breastfeeding requires information and ongoing support. Lay counselors and community-based groups could provide this information and support. This way we could save money, plastic, machinery, rubber, glass, trees, metal, and at the same time we would create new jobs.

Daycare is another environmental inefficiency. I realize full well that many women have no choice about using daycare and that others select daycare as the best choice. However, without presuming to judge, I can say that daycare is not the ideal solution to the work and family counterpoint.

First, direct payments to parents are much more efficient than subsidies to institutions. Daycare involves two separate facilities for the care of one child. One is empty during the day; and the other is empty at night. Daycare creates new child-rearing expenses: salaries, utilities, rent, transportation, clothing, single-use diapers, lunch bags, and prepackaged food and drinks.

Then, too, while arguing about what type of daycare is best, we neglect to ask the important underlying questions: Is the work of raising the children and managing the home distributed fairly among family members? Do we as a society value childrearing enough to provide financial support for it? Have we exhausted our ability to create better childcare choices? Are we willing to learn from existing job descriptions and work environments that *are* responsive to children's needs? Can we learn anything from other countries about how *they* support families? Are we willing to take care of our own children? Will we take care of those children whose parents do not or cannot care for them?

You don't need a lot of paraphernalia for your baby, and what you do need can be chosen from products and services that are helpful to the earth. You can choose a low-technology birth in a place you feel safe. You can breastfeed your baby for as long as you both feel comfortable. You can feed your baby from your own table—simple, fresh foods that are ground or mashed by hand. You can dress your baby in natural, nonexploitive materials. You can use cloth diapers. You can look for creative ways to incorporate your baby into your life, and examine any separation between work and family to see if it returns more energy than it uses up. You can take care of your baby yourself. Think low-use energy products *and processes*, but do not think scarcity. Be creative and open-minded, and be especially wary of products and processes that overly complicate your life or that offer you something for nothing.

The best-kept secret in the world may be that we *do* know how to raise healthy children. We don't hear enough about it, however, because no one has the market on it and because some of us think it is harder than it really is. Raising healthy children is a profound environmental contribution. The human infant is engineered to seek health and knows what he or she needs. We can respond to our children rather than to the experts. If we follow the cues of the present child rather than the mistakes of the past, we have a good chance of raising human beings who care, who do not exploit people or things out of pride or avarice. And if we raise human beings who care, then everything else will take care of itself.

Is This the Beginning or the End?

Recent events in the Middle East give us cause for concern. It is difficult to reconcile these events with others occurring in other parts of the world, where representatives of diverse philosophical and political systems have been able to reach agreements thought impossible only a few years ago. Will the increasing goodwill of the world community make it possible for the Middle Eastern events to be resolved in a new way also? Can we understand the dramatic movement underfoot in the world as a whole?

Two parallel paths are unfolding simultaneously at this time. One faces the excesses and poor judgments of the past, bears responsibility for them, and works to heal them. Another creates new and better choices for the future. It reminds me of the recovery process. Is the world in recovery? I recognize in the highs and lows of world events the same ebbs and flows that I have come to identify in myself as I have healed my own past—ebbs and flows that are characteristic of day-to-day emotional life in a healthy state.

Is it the dawn of the new century that causes us to vacillate between paradise and destruction? The nineties will challenge our hopefulness unless we understand the basic transformative nature of the times. The great religious celebrations of Resurrection and Passover remind us that death is always followed by rebirth. Winter is followed by spring. Death gives new life to the living. Darkest hours come just before new light.

Some would suggest naïveté or lack of real concern among those who prefer to see hope rather than despair in the world. To me, there is no choice. I believe in the perfectibility of the human spirit, and world events, both by reason and design, mimic personal transformation. We are burning off the dross of human experience. If birth is a metaphor for life, then there is no new life without labor. During those New Year's Eve peace meditations of the late eighties, we put out a call for transformation, and we are now reaping the harvest.

I am hopeful today because of the children and the men. My thoughts can focus on crack babies and AIDS babies and Romanian babies, and I am glad that their plight has been brought to public awareness and that help is on the way. I do not see these babies in my daily life, however. What I see in my daily life is another story.

I see babies whose emotional needs are being met—babies who are carried all the time and who are suckled with the milk of their own species, free of charge and without pollutants, additives, or preservatives. Nearly 50 percent of our readers— over 75,000 women—breastfeed their babies for two years. Twenty-seven percent breastfeed their babies for three to five years. Whereas statistics on the number of children in daycare are rising daily, nearly 50 percent of *Mothering*'s readers are full-time parents. Even though rumor has it that the traditional family is dead, 87 percent of our readers live in two-parent households.

I see fathers who have changed. In the parenting workshops I have been doing at Omega Institute these past six years, I have witnessed profound changes in parenting beliefs. Men who first came to Omega, often cajoled by their wives and incredulous of information based on experience rather than on experts and references, are now active and independent participants.

Men, in general, are changing. Robert Bly, a contemporary spokesperson for men, reminds us in his PBS interview with

Bill Moyers that men have their own unique needs in a relationship, just as women do. Austin-based men's magazine *Man!* is a popular vehicle for man-to-man communication. Six years ago, it was uncommon for men to share emotional experiences with other men. Today, groups of men are meeting all over the country to do just that.

The parallel path that gives me hope is the one feeding the underbelly of international events. Men, women, couples, and children are all choosing a new way, and are willing to handle the ambivalence of life lived without the controls thought necessary in the past. Also along this path, despite our fears of an unknowable future, we keep having children, building families, and starting over day after day.

Perhaps biology is stronger than psychology and tricks the mind into thinking it is in charge while it is the heart that really leads. Every day more volunteers sign up for a job that requires hope. *Wanted: Men and women to volunteer for a job in which no experience is required, no predictability or control is possible. This job demands long hours and offers no pay, no training, and little praise. Society will hold incredibly high standards for this job, but will give little support to it. Everyone else in society will think they know how to do the job better than you, yet you will be the only one blamed if something goes wrong. This is a totally improvisational position.* This is the job of being a parent.

I am hopeful because every day people volunteer for this job and, in fact, bring a whole new dimension to it—even an entirely new job description. *Wanted: Men and women to volunteer for a job developing the thinking and emotional capacity of an entire generation. Potential to inexorably affect the quality of life on the planet. Potential to improve the environment, ensure world peace, and eliminate nuclear war. This job is unlike any other and yet will prepare you for anything. Has been known to shake up chakras and hasten enlightenment. Value of job is beyond money, so payment is made in memories, self-esteem, and personal growth. Individuals handpicked for the position.*

Whether our times herald the beginning or the end may depend not so much on events in the Middle East, the Soviet Union, and Berlin, but rather on how many people sign up for the latter job and take seriously the imparting of affection, empathy, and trust. The imparting of conscience. How many will be ambassadors of hope? Who will emotionally prepare future generations to live in a world where none are too hungry, too greedy, or too repressed? Children who have witnessed their parents tackle personal transformation will have much to bring to a world we can only imagine. Stand tall, parents. We hold the future in our hands. Grab hold of Hope. We're her favorites, and she's been on vacation for a long time.

Coming of Age in America

Today I watched my teenage son and two of his friends run barefoot out to the hammock. It's early fall and cold, and the way to the hammock is rocky; but I could tell it was important to them to do it, to know they could run barefoot over the rocks. The boys have also been camping out on our land the last two nights. The first night, they braved three hours in the tent while the worst thunder and lightning storm of the season crashed outside. Later, when they finally came soaked into the house, they admitted that the water had been running under the tent and dripping in their faces, but as they jokingly said, they endured it because they were "being men."

Even though they are aware of what is happening to them, these boys are living out a rite of passage. While many may complain that our modern lives are devoid of meaningful rituals, I am confident that young people will invent those rituals they need to come of age in the United States today.

The popular press tends to portray teens in a negative way. A recent *Newsweek* special edition on adolescence gives the impression that most teens are experimenting with drugs, alcohol, and sex, and are overly concerned with fashion and vulgar music. Sound familiar? Of course, it does. But just who are these teens? Am I naïve because I live in a small town, or is the prevailing stereotype simply another generation's way of trivializing and condescending to the teen experience? The truth is that teens *are* too much for most people to handle—not because they are into drugs, sex, and fashion, but because they reflect so clearly the inconsistencies and ambiguities of adult life.

Adults and teens are involved in an intimate transfer of power. Alternately, teens grab for power, then refuse it.

Alternately, we are eager to give it up and jealous of its loss. This is the stuff of the adolescent years. It cannot be avoided by better parenting. In fact, to avoid it may be to assure difficulty with power and authority later in life.

We *need* a fresh look at teens. At a time when children require clear direction and moral leadership from us, we often dismiss their behavior as merely a product of overactive hormones, or avoid asserting our authority for fear of confrontation. And we are arrogant. As a generation of parents who have tried to be conscious mothers and fathers and who remember the pain of our own childhoods, we have allowed ourselves to believe that if we parented "right," our children would be spared the turmoil of the teen years. And we have judged harshly those families who have had trouble with their teens, believing that such problems could be avoided through virtuous parenting. What we often fail to understand is that the power struggle between teens and adults is necessary for the child to become an adult. It goes with the territory.

The parent-child relationship during adolescence resembles the weaning process of the bear cub. The mother bear is a devoted mother and teaches her cubs to obey her unconditionally. One day, she takes her cubs to a tree and, in effect, tells them to climb up it and not to come down under any circumstances. Then the mother bear leaves and never comes back. In order to survive, the bear cubs have to disobey their mother.

In the United States today, we are confused about disobedience. On one hand, we disapprove of the often harmless rebellion manifested by teen clothes, hairstyles, and music. On the other hand, we are ineffectual in responding to the more dangerous temptations of drugs, alcohol, sex, and suicide. We need a new look at teens because we need to better understand the adolescent experience. Then we can stop taking their behavior personally and can respond to our teenagers as the elders they expect us to be.

Teens are like two year olds. They have excellent boundaries.

Remember the dance teacher who tells the little ones to imagine a balloon around each dancer, separating them from the others? Teens know about this balloon. They know what is their business and what is yours. They have a healthy narcissism; they know their preferences, and reasoning cannot change their minds. And they are highly self-conscious. Often it's as if they've just wakened from a dream and realized that they are here. This is why many teens go through a black phase in the early teen years. For a while, they dye their hair black and wear black lipstick and nail polish, black T-shirts, and long, black coats. They are in hiding.

Teens also have a healthy rebelliousness. For the first time, they see the life of their family with some degree of objectivity. They then have to reconcile this new knowledge with their love for their family and their growing attachment to their peers. They are not quite sure who they are, but they are absolutely sure of who they are not. They are creating themselves.

This teen rebelliousness is often difficult for parents to deal with because it challenges them at a time when they may be in a state of flux themselves. Adolescence runs parallel to "middle-essence," a time when parents may be reevaluating their own lives. The teens are thrusting outward; the parents are looking inward. The teens want to embellish; the parents to simplify. This counterpoint is probably necessary. It keeps the parents from getting too introspective and serious, and it keeps the teens with their feet on the ground.

The other day, I spoke to a father who said his four year old was a brat because she took forever to put away her toys and she talked back to him. "But she's supposed to be a brat," I thought. Teens are brats, too. And they're supposed to be. They are stubborn, intractable, rude, unaware of others' needs, difficult to talk to, and emotionally volatile. In short, they have excellent boundaries. It is precisely these emerging boundaries, so well defined, that we adults find infuriating. We are used to and much prefer acquiescence from our children. We believe that giving in to other people is kinder than resistance, and we hope we have raised our children to be kind. The wise parent will encourage this healthy boundary development. At the same time, he or she will set limits and provide structure—in an effort to reflect what real life is like and to balance the unlimited possibilities the teen feels inside.

It is in understanding and having compassion for the teen experience that we adults can best respond to it. The teen years are necessarily a time of upheaval. This upheaval is part of the transformation from child to adult and from dependence to independence. The teen is neither child nor adult; the teen is in "nor" time. In nor time, all is experienced with a sense of heightened awareness. The protective veil of the family parts a bit, and the teen sees that there is a discrepancy between what people say and what they do. This loss of innocence begins the unfolding of awareness so vital to the emerging adult. And consciousness is never won without suffering. Despite the teen's changes of mood and lack of response, wise parents continue to act as bumper rails on the bridge that their child drives across.

Parenting is mostly strategy. You hope for some modicum of control, but also know that anything can happen. When our children are babies, there is only so far they can go, and our world with them seems finite. When they are teens, our world with them is infinite. We see our teens as vulnerable; they feel invincible. We think of teens as *having arrived* somewhere, when in fact, it has just occurred to them that they are *going* somewhere. Having discovered this, they want to get to that "somewhere" as soon as possible. We begin to realize that we can no longer protect them all the time, and that we will have to learn to live without them sooner than we thought.

Being a parent of a teen requires great reserves of confidence, self-esteem, and resiliency—if for no other reason than to be able to confront six tall young men in a messy kitchen and demand that they clean it up. Being a parent of a teen requires a willingness to claim your authority as a parent and to insist on the right and responsibility to protect your child even when he or she does not want protection. And being a parent of a teen requires developing a sense of humor. Life with teens can be very funny. As Dorothy Parker said, "The best way to keep children home is make the home atmosphere pleasant—and let the air out of the tires."

Holy Mother

The gross national product does not include the beauty of our poetry or the strength of our marriages, the intelligence of our public debate or the integrity of our public officials. It allows neither for the justice in our courts, nor for the justness of our dealings with each other.

The gross national product measures our wit not our courage, neither our wisdom nor our learning, neither our compassion nor our devotion to country. It measures everything, in short, except that which makes life worthwhile.

—Robert Kennedy

We know what our gross national product is. What is our gross national process? How are we doing? Do we value the intangible—and invisible—processes of life? While our nation is in furor loquendi about daycare subsidies and school restructuring, wouldn't we achieve a lot by simply learning to value parenting and teaching again? As long as the value of parenting and teaching is subject to economic standards and variables, we cannot. We've got things backwards. It is the health of everyday processes that keeps us feeling good and doing our best, and doing our best results in a healthy economy.

What are healthy processes? Kennedy identified some: the marital process, the intellectual process, and the political process. We have grave doubts in our society today about these particular processes as well as others. Ellen Goodman entitled her October 2, 1990, column "Bad Case of Jitters Afflicts

Americans." It's almost as if we *want* a recession to give living proof of how bad we feel. We don't know how things got this way, and we've forgotten that we're in charge.

It is time to give birth to a new economy and a new world order that values process and understands the correct balance between quantity and quality, goods and services. Valuing the products of life over the processes of life is a recent human aberration. Before the clock, time was measured by the natural rhythms of the days and the seasons. Ample evidence suggests that people, too, have natural rhythms and times of being inherently more productive. It was the move to industrialization that began to compete with activities of intangible, intrinsic worth. Eventually, the seduction of materialism lured us away from even scheduling in such activities.

Some people associate a product-valued economy with a patriarchal system, in which values are traditionally linked to the masculine *as symbol*. Similarly, one can associate a process-valued economy with the feminine *as symbol*. We live in a society, however, that romanticizes and trivializes the feminine, and holds as the ideal of feminine beauty women who look like adolescent males with breasts. And we live in an economy that regards women as cheap labor. In the marketplace, women work for less than men. At home, we do the large majority of the work. I believe that we enslave ourselves.

Is it any wonder, then, that we have not successfully resolved the childcare debate? Child care and national family policy are process issues, and thus sexist issues. Women themselves engage in sexism when they debate the either/or dichotomy of work or home. Too often, we do not realize the devaluation involved in playing by the crumbling rules of a male-dominated society rather than making up our own. The matriarchal process-based model comes from a religious belief system in which the Divine is immanent, within life, within us, ascribing sacredness to the ordinary processes of daily life. Rather than choosing between the opposites, let us evolve a culture that values

both the product *and* the process, a culture that synthesizes both
the patriarchy and the matriarchy.

To do this, we must appreciate the beauty of the mature
woman, the woman as mother. Pregnancy and birth are matu-
ration processes for women. And yet, we often find ourselves
yearning for the prepregnant body and the youthful skin, while
disdaining the stretch marks and full stomachs that are the visible signs of our courage. We must learn to love the body of a
mature woman, to take the cultural norm inside and transform
it. And we must put all of our loves—work *and* family, mothering *and* career, self *and* others—on the bargaining table at once,
and not assume that because we are women, we must acquiesce
to the cultural ideal. To run our personal lives in enslavement to
an economic reality that does not serve our needs makes society
crazy.

How do we learn to value the feminine—the mature woman,
the home-cooked meals, the moments by the fire, the taking
care of one another? Science lends a hand. The DNA mitochon-
drial research of biochemist Alan C. Wilson traces all ancestral
lines back to a single mother, who probably lived in Africa over
200,000 years ago. We really are one family. And the Goddess
who is in life, who is part of life, and who gives life is as valuable as the God who transcends it.

For the last several hundred years, it has been dangerous to
be a woman. For the last 30 years, it has been confusing. But
between 30,000 BC and 2,000 BC, to be a woman was to be a
Goddess. Archeological and anthropological evidence attest to
the sacredness of the everyday feminine processes of life in
times past.

Aphrodite (Venus) was considered the Goddess of birth.
Artemis (Diana) was considered the Goddess of midwifery.
Women were the first artists, the first herbalists, the first heal-
ers, the first shamans, the first magicians. Women developed
architecture and agriculture (around 10,000 BC). Enheduanna,
an Egyptian priestess of the moon goddess Artemis, was the

first writer (around 1,000 BC).

We need to regain our reverence for life—a reverence that has been overshadowed by our love of materialism, our fear of death, and our fascination with problems. We speak with forked tongues. Our personal needs and passions fuel us, but we don't fight for them. Instead, we trade them in for cancer. We subjugate them to larger societal ideals, never realizing that the creation—and the transformation—of these models are direct results of our choices and our bottom lines. *We are our culture.*

The sacred Christian image of the feminine is the Blessed Virgin, one who transcends both sexuality and death. The virgin *as symbol* is just *one* aspect of the feminine. Let us celebrate others. Let us resurrect an ancient image of the feminine, one that is part of everyday life, within us, accessible through daily experience, corpulent, dirty, wise, and fierce.

Once we see the mother as holy again and recognize both her sacred and mundane import in society, the smaller questions of social and economic merit will take care of themselves. We have the key to unlock the future, and we don't even know it. . . . Start today. Start by listening to your body (go to the bathroom the *first* time you have the urge), following a hunch, believing in magic, letting things happen, noticing the process, moving indirectly. Start by honoring the feminine impulse within you whether you are a man or a woman. Put a foot forward into the mystery. Feel what happens.

Like a Weaning

I'd like to write about babies because I know that many of you have babies, but I don't. I have teens, and I want to scream. I think it may have to do with being short. Maybe if I were a taller parent. . . . Maybe if I were a married parent. . . . Maybe if. . . . Where have we gotten the idea that we can control human beings? Why do we believe our virtue and good intentions can create perfect children? Which one of us was a perfect child? One analyst I know says she sees more "perfect children" in her chair than those who raised hell.

Something about parenting teens is reminiscent of the early years of parenting. Things are all askew, and you feel as if you've arrived in a foreign land where you certainly don't know the territory and haven't yet learned the language. The things that used to work don't work anymore, and you suddenly realize that you got more than you bargained for. And, no one talks about it. Not really. Not the scary stuff. We're all afraid it might be our fault.

When they are babies, you can keep their outrageous behavior to yourself. You don't have to tell anyone that your daughter cut her hair with pinking shears and then shut her baby brother up in the toy chest. And you don't have to mention what you did when you found out. The behavior of teens is a much more public affair.

Your friends see your teens downtown in black, playing cool with cigarettes. Your coworkers report on your teens' driving prowess. Other parents form alliances to report teen drug and alcohol transgressions. Your daughter's friend's mother calls in the middle of the night to say that someone you thought you knew very well has just climbed out of her window. The authorities arrest teens for shoplifting just to give them a taste of jail. Therapist friends suggest addiction counseling for things you suspect may just be normal experimentation. You wonder if in this self-obsessed, antiseptic society, teens have a right to experiment anymore. You wonder about teen bashing. But you're not sure. And you worry.

Then you look at your teens. These are the same sweet children you have loved and trusted over the years. The ones you have intimate communication with. The ones you have, in fact, learned relationship with. You have always trusted them. You have spent years building trust with them. Do you stop trusting them now because the temptations are greater, the risks riskier? Can you afford to let them learn through their own experience —the way you learned, the way anything important is learned when the risks are so great and when you don't have any other choice anyway?

When they were little, you worried about them falling into the swimming pool. You breathed a sigh of relief when they all learned to swim. Now you worry about the whole ocean. There are cars. New Mexico has the highest rate of drunken driving in the country. Car accidents are the leading cause of death among teens. There are cigarettes. You wonder about a society that sells something more addictive than heroin in vending machines. You worry about drugs. Are they really available in schoolyards? You worry about food. How can anyone live long on Hershey's Kisses, orange soda, and potato chips? Why don't they remember to take their vitamins? No wonder they're coughing.

I talked recently to a woman whose name you would know. She spoke in hushed tones about her marriage and her teens. The whole thing was going to hell in a handbasket, but she was not specific. I'm sure she was afraid to tell me, Ms. Perfect Parent, what was really happening. I was dying to tell her what was really happening here. Like in the early days of parenting, we keep our pain and confusion to ourselves, fearing that confiding in others will confirm our fears of inadequacy.

It helps me to talk to other parents of teens, and especially to talk to parents of grown children. I cried with relief over an article by Eda LeShan about little monsters who grew up to be rabbis and attorneys. I was ecstatic when my neighbor told me about the five foreign cars his grown daughter had wrecked when she was a teen. And I laughed uproariously when this same neighbor described the time he came upon his teenage son smoking and playing pinball in a local convenience store. My neighbor calmly walked over to him and had a casual conversation while his son hid the burning cigarette in his pocket. I feel comforted when I hear that passive-aggressive and manic-depressive are normal in the teen years. My favorite reassurance is that the closer you've been with your child, the harder the teen years are. I wouldn't have believed that earlier, when I could still control their behavior, but it makes sense now.

It makes sense now because I understand what is happening. The teen years are like a weaning. Although we still love these children as we did when we held them in our arms, *they must leave us.* And for them to leave us with their self-esteem intact, they must sometimes fight their way out. At eight or nine, they assure us that they will live with us forever—or at most, build their own house right next door to ours. We are all relieved. This, however, is not what is best for them. They must sometimes fight their way out.

This summer I will have three teenagers. Send money, flowers, condolences. Pray that I don't take to drink. I've taught them excellent boundaries, and now they are using them against me. They've caught me at my game. They are better at it than I am. They challenge me to trust them. And trust is, after all, all that I have.

I have raised my children to have certain values, and now it is time for them to test and make them their own. I have tried to shield them from society; they want to jump in feetfirst. And yet, I hold on tight. Unlike some parents who seem to abandon their children once they become teens and attribute to them more worldly experience than they could have, I do not. I am only the bumper rails, though. They are now in the driver's seat, and the air is low in the tires, and they have little experience with snow and ice, and they are in the hands of God.

These are the same teens who sometimes still want to get in bed with me after a bad illness or a stressful week. The same teens who demonstrate against the war in the Middle East and in support of higher teacher salaries. The same teens who work weekly with the homeless. The same teens who have intense loyalty to their friends and compassionate tolerance of intolerant adults. The same teens who hold a baby with the tenderness of Mother Teresa.

I am on a roller coaster of my own creation. I have no choice but to hold on. I am a parent of teens, and I do not know the way. They bring out the worst in me and have seen my best. All else that has come before in our relationship—the sleepless nights, the hospital stays, the tantrums, and the rocking chair—has prepared me for this trusting. For no one else would I hang on so tightly with one hand while I loosen the grip of my longing with the other.

The Way Back Home

I look around me these days and wonder what on earth is going on. The news abounds with stories of conflict and upheaval, and most people I talk to offer up either a conspiracy or a doom theory as explanation. I would offer a counterproposal. What the world is going through in the latter part of the 20th century is akin to what the individual goes through in the process of individuation. In order to stop being *more* than what we are, and be simply *what we are*, we must address the dark side of our nature, the underbelly of our lives. We must bring up the demons, look them in the eye, and integrate them. Likewise, countries mimic this individuation process when they really begin to seek self-determination.

I do not fear the international political upheavals because my own personal experience tells me that once one has gone to hell, one can be reborn. And one is reborn a richer, more complex, and wilder person. The world needs a few more wild people now—people who are originals, people who are in the habit of dredging deeply into their complexity and sharing it with others.

Those of us who have given birth to ourselves know that the experience of individuation can feel on the inside the way political upheaval looks on the outside. This individuation runs parallel to the explosive and outrageous behavior we see all around us today on the world stage. And because both this personal and this political process of individuation cannot by nature be measured, predicted, or controlled, it can be terrifying. Terror is the counterpoint to ecstasy, and ecstasy is something that is pushing to be reborn in the world.

The hysteria over the way things are is manifested in grief over the death of the family. We often believe that things were better before, in the past, when certain values were intact. We lose faith in the future and in our own human perfectibility. The family *is* dead, and it is a good thing.

The root of the word *family* means "in service to the father." What about the mother? Not only is family no longer in service to the father, in some families there is no father and that, too, is OK. A family that is in service to *any one member* over another is a family that is in service to the dominator model of behavior, a model we are moving away from as we embrace the partner-ship model.

Authoritarian families no longer work. Authoritarian govern-ments no longer work. People all over the world, both in soci-eties and in families, are seeking self-determination. Family is more than a place; it is a system. This system may include a wife, husband, and children. It may include lovers, best friends, favorite aunts, and old friends. It may include same-sex com-panions and next-door neighbors. And it may change. It can't be locked in. The family system, as it is of our own creation, contains us rather than controls us. Families of the new order are comprised of individuals bound together not by duty or custom, but by freely chosen mutual respect and admiration.

The family is dead because the old family was based on myths that no longer feed us. One such myth is the myth of perfection. The perfect family dressed up in crinolines and patent leather shoes, never got mad, and sought superiority over other families through accomplishments. We know too much now about what *really* went on behind the closed doors of those perfect families to buy into that myth anymore.

A second myth is the myth of domination. Parents dominate over children. The father dominates over the mother. This no longer works. What now works is a cooperative model, a win-win consensus in which all persuasions are put out on the table and all family members share in the decision making.

Yet a third myth is the good parents/good children myth. A subset of this myth is the belief that bad things do not happen to good people. Of course, they do. Good parents do not necessarily create good children. Children create themselves out of the complex mix of temperament, environment, and loving care. And while the original parent-child relationship is essential to the development of trust, empathy, and attachment, we know many children with nothing who somehow make it, and others with everything who do not. Love remains a mystery.

We have also accepted the myth that marriage is a fixed contract rather than a fluid process, and we continually bemoan divorce statistics that we might be celebrating. Never before in history have men and women really told each other who they are and what they want in relationship. The new reality tells us that relationships between men and women, like relationships between parents and children, cannot be measured, predicted, or controlled.

When we let the old model of family and marriage die, we begin to see all other people as brothers and sisters, and invest all our human interactions with trust and compassion. And we become willing to love those family members who are not like us and with whom we do not agree. We begin to know unconditional love.

We have carried a misperception of the family as a place to show off our trophies and awards, to brag about our accomplishments, and to be number one. And while we sometimes want to do these things, binding together through our desire to be more than what we are separates us from others and denies the complexity of our own humanity. Family is not where we are perfect. Family is where we can fall apart.

Sometimes when we return to our families of origin, the skeletons come out of the closet to surprise us. Where else can they come out? So much comes up. So much dirty laundry. We don't have anything to hide anymore. We know about starvation, cruelty, AIDS, incest, political oppression, and human suffering.

Human suffering has always been with us. It always will be. It comes with the territory.

To romanticize the human condition and believe we can control it is to not suffer the suffering, to not be fully human, to not know the ecstasy that is on the other side of this suffering. And while I do not advocate passion without mercy, neither do I condone the self-indulgence that embraces only what I approve of or understand about life.

The old world order of control, domination, and supremacy is crumbling. Us versus Them, Win or Lose, Either/Or are all on the way out. The demons are coming out of the closet, and we are running to meet them.

The new world order is one of intuition, process, cooperation, and partnership—we all win. We are finding our way back home, not by erecting a bigger and more idealistic edifice of family, but by collapsing into what family has always been. A place where we can fall apart. A place where the worst in us can act out, where we can suck our thumbs, where we can hide in the bathroom. Family is the place where the strangest people live, a place where we can hold onto one another and come in from the cold.

About the Author

Peggy O'Mara (44) is the mother of four children: Lally (17), Finnie (15), Bram (13), and Nora (9). She is a poet and has been the publisher and editor of *Mothering* since 1980. She and her family live in Santa Fe, New Mexico.

About MOTHERING

"Some of the magazines devoted to child-raising often seem like they have a secret agenda to co-opt you into buying expensive trinkets for Junior. Not so with *Mothering*. This excellent Santa Fe quarterly offers a holistic approach toward life with your child *and* with the planet."

—*USA Today*

"Mom and dad could both use a little *Mothering*. . . . a calm, simple service-oriented look at how to raise children in an often confusing world. When you read the magazine, you know its editors care."

—*Magazine Week*

"You don't have to be a mother to read *Mothering*. Take a look even if you're only interested in seeing tomorrow's leaders grow up healthy, secure, and loved. *Mothering* covers the waterfront with its parent-tested lore on everything from toilet training to teenage turmoil. And its discussions of family living lend uncanny insight into dealing with non-family members in the workplace and the community."

—*Utne Reader, announcing* Mothering *as the winner of the 1990 Alternative Press Award for Service Journalism*

For subscription information, please call—

1-800-545-9364

Other books from *Mothering* include:

Vaccinations

Circumcision

Schooling at Home: Parents, Kids, and Learning

Being a Father: Family, Work, and Self

Midwifery and the Law

Teens: A Fresh Look

Write for a free catalog of current publications—

Mothering, PO Box 1690, Santa Fe, NM 87504